TOP MAN

About the Author

Don G. Mitchell is vice-chairman of the Marriott Corporation and executive committee chairman of the American Management Association. He was educated at the University of Cincinnati and the University of Florida.

Mr. Mitchell has been board chairman of General Time Corporation, president of General Telephone and Electronics Corporation, and board chairman of Sylvania Electric Products, Inc. He is currently a board member of ACF Industries, Inc.; American Motors Corporation; CPC International Corporation; Electronic Memories and Magnetics, Inc.; International Milling Company, Inc.; Irving Trust Company; Massachusetts Mutual Life Insurance Company; and National Biscuit Company.

Mr. Mitchell was long-time board chairman of AMA before assuming his present position as executive committee chairman, and he is a frequent lecturer before management groups.

TOP MAN

Reflections of a Chief Executive

Don G. Mitchell

American Management Association

To
Lawrence A. Appley
who has been my colleague in
management education for more than 30 years

Preface

Over the past ten years it has been my privilege to attend as a guest lecturer literally dozens of conferences of corporation presidents in the United States, Canada, Mexico, and most of the countries of Europe.

These were management courses for presidents and presidents' round tables put on by The Presidents Association—an affiliate of the American Management Association.

The average attendance at these meetings was about 35, the average duration about five days. The subject: How to Do a Better Job of Managing.

It is, of course, impossible to attend these meetings time after time without learning much more than one gives.

One thing, however, over the years impressed itself on my consciousness and gradually evolved into a major theme of my lectures. This was that the majority of these corporation presidents were giving most of their attention to the techniques of management and too often forgetting the fundamentals.

In these days of rapid change, the techniques of management are changing so fast and so often that it is almost impossible to keep up with them. The fundamentals, however, are just as solid as ever and neither technological explosion nor electronic computers have changed them or are likely to in the foreseeable future.

Over the years hundreds of these executives have asked me if I would put down on paper some of the thinking that has developed out of these discussions, and this book is an attempt to do so.

I am a lecturer, not a writer, and I am sure these ideas would never have found their way into print if my friend Graef (Bud) Crystal of Booz, Allen & Hamilton Inc. had not made me sit down in front of a tape recorder for days while he fired questions at me.

Somehow, out of this process, this book evolved. The ideas and the responsibility for them are mine—many of the words are Bud's.

Contents

I	Introduction	11
II	Establishing the Goals	17
III	Organization	29
IV	Decentralization and Delegation	38
V	Selecting Your Team	48
VI	Developing Your People	69
VII	Controlling the Organization	80
VIII	Communication	98
IX	Compensation	109
X	The Corporate Staff	134
XI	The President's Job	142
XII	The Board of Directors	157
XIII	Personal Financial Planning	164
XIV	The Broader View of Management	172
XV	Management's Challenges for the Future	179
	Index	187

I
Introduction

Over the past few years literally hundreds of books have been published on virtually every aspect of management. Given enough free time and a strong pair of eyes, the reader can learn how PERT can save him from making a drastic mistake; how sensitivity training (and a good mouthwash) can make him more effective in managing his fellow workers; how, if all else fails, the computer will save his foundering enterprise.

Each of these authors is a specialist in his field, and each views the management process through his own very specialized eyes.

Now, this is not to say that books on PERT, sensitivity training, computers, and the like are not valuable management aids. These books admirably describe what I like to call the applications of management. They do not deal, however, with the fundamentals—or, if you will, the principles—of management. That is the basic purpose of this book.

The fundamentals of management, like the fundamentals of all other fields, have one thing in common: You must not violate them if you wish to succeed. They are the bedrock—the foundation—on which the field of management is built. If you have ever built a house (or spent sufficient time as a sidewalk superintendent), you know that the foundation of a split-level is virtually identical to the foundation of a saltbox colonial. Certainly, the shape may differ, but the way in which the foundation is laid, the materials that are used—these are the same. And so it is with management. If you build a good foundation with good fundamentals, you can load a great variety of designs or applications on top of it. But the most sophisticated design is bound to collapse if the foundation is not sound.

The fundamentals of management, like the fundamentals of all other fields, have another thing in common: There aren't very many of them. It is of some significance that Moses didn't come down from Mount Sinai with the "Five Hundred Commandments." All it took was ten. And a number of these were further distilled into what we popularly call the Golden Rule.

The fundamentals of management, like the fundamentals of all other fields, have a third thing in common: They are simple in appearance but, for some reason, are awfully hard to learn. You watch the stonemason laying a foundation, and you think, "What a snap! All the guy does is dig a hole and pour some concrete." At least, that's the way I viewed it until I tried to lay a foundation myself. Like the people who built the Leaning Tower of Pisa, I soon learned there is something more to laying a foundation than digging a hole and pouring some concrete.

Early in my career, I had to learn management fundamentals the hard way. Of course I knew about them, but, like motherhood and saluting the flag, they were rather homely virtues. It was much more fun to consider the intricacies of double declining depreciation and the glories of multicolored production charts. After a number of false starts, however, I came to realize that I could use an infinite variety of applications, and, provided that I was reasonably prudent, any of them would work. At the same time I came to realize that, if I violated even one fundamental of management, I was bound to fail.

Have you ever considered why two companies which use diametrically opposite management applications are both successful? One swears by psychological tests in selecting good people; the other scorns such modern tomfoolery. One has a performance appraisal form that is fully two yards long; the other uses a simple one-page form. Yet both companies are immensely profitable. Obviously, it is not psychological tests or the length of the performance appraisal form that accounts for this success. Certainly, well-designed applications can be of some help, but ultimately these companies are successful because they both follow certain management fundamentals.

Before going any further, let us consider what we mean by management. Reduced to its simplest form, management is the act of accomplishing work through other people. Everyone who has at least one person reporting directly to him, over whom he has the power of hiring and firing, is a manager. (I am often amused to find staff people who are called Manager of "X," but have not one subordinate. These people may be managing a function, but they are not managers.) A man may abdicate his managerial responsibilities or discharge them poorly, but as long as he has people reporting to him he still remains a manager.

All managers are basically alike, and all must use the same management fundamentals if they are to succeed. From the standpoint of management fundamentals there is no essential difference between the lowest-level foreman, who has six factory workers reporting to him, and the president of a huge corporation, who has 750,000 employees under his jurisdiction.

When asked about their career choices, young college graduates are likely to respond, "I'm going into sales management" or "I'm going into personnel management." To these would-be leaders, there is a great difference between sales management and personnel management. In fact, there is no difference.

Certainly, each has to learn the mechanics of differing fields, and each has to become adept at using the latest "buzz words," but these do not add up to *man-*

agement. For management is a discipline unto itself, and the fundamentals of management apply to any field.

It is not an overstatement, in my opinion, to say that *he who can truly manage can manage anything*. He can manage a bank, he can manage a railroad, he can manage a manufacturing business, and—as much as anyone can—he can even manage the government. The art of being a good manager is portable.

The concept that a good manager can manage anything is certainly not original with me. Until recently, however, it has been relatively unproven, for putting it into practice required a degree of faith that most executives seemed to lack. The thought of moving a good personnel manager into the sales manager's job, although theoretically sound, seemed, from a practical standpoint, only to invite disaster. The thought of hiring a good bank manager to run a manufacturing plant was even more foreign.

In the past few years, however, business has begun to be caught in a crunch between an exponentially growing demand for capable management talent and a rather limited supply of such talent. In fact, the supply is going to dwindle over the next decade as the "depression babies" reach the age range from which middle and top managers are selected. Those executives who a few years ago wouldn't give the personnel manager the sales manager's job—on very pragmatic grounds—are now making such switches with greater frequency, and on the very same pragmatic grounds. They don't have enough good managers, and so they have no choice but to try new approaches, transferring managers from one discipline to another and (heaven forbid!) bringing in managers from completely foreign industries who can't even spell the names of the new products they are handling, much less recognize them.

It has come as something of a surprise to these skeptical and pragmatic executives that their transplants, after a very short transition period, blossom once again into excellent managers. It comes as no surprise to those of us who believe that a good manager can manage anything.

*　　*　　*　　*

In the chapters that follow, the reader should keep in mind that the activities of management are a continuous, ongoing process, and not necessarily a sequential one, as might be implied by the order of topics covered. For example, a manager in an existing organization is continuously defining his goals, organizing his team, delegating responsibilities, selecting and developing managers, controlling their activities, and compensating them. Nevertheless, one must break into this continuous circle at some point to begin the discussion of management fundamentals. Therefore, I have chosen to start with the establishment of organization goals and to orient the succeeding chapters in a manner which reflects the general order of events that would occur in the establishment of a totally new company.

II

Establishing the Goals

*M*anagement is not an end in itself. It is rather a means to an end. For "end," substitute the word "goal."

The first thing that a manager has to do is know where he is going. The goal of some managers is very simple: *more.* They want more sales, more profit, more of anything that is good for their business. Having established this, they consider themselves finished with goal setting and free to concentrate on the "real" aspects of running a business.

These managers have not established a goal in any sense of the word. "More" only fixes the direction in which the manager wishes to head. It says nothing about *how far* he plans to travel and the *time* he intends to take in getting there. These are the twin factors which create a *true* goal.

So the first thing any good manager must do is to

establish a goal at which he can aim the efforts of his team and against which he can measure the efficacy of these efforts. To be more precise, the good manager must really establish two goals. The first of these is a short-range goal: what his team is going to accomplish this year. The second is a longer-range goal: what his team is going to accomplish five to ten years from now. One goal complements the other, and neither can exist independently.

Popes of the Roman Catholic Church occasionally name cardinals *in pectore*—that is, "in their hearts." The names of these cardinals are not divulged to the public, and sometimes even the individual so honored is not informed of his designation as cardinal. There is a third goal that I believe a good manager should formulate, and like the Popes I believe that goal should be *in pectore*. I like to call this a dream goal. It is that goal which you don't really expect to achieve but which, in your Walter Mitty ruminations, you would love to achieve. Maybe that goal is to make your company the largest or the most profitable in the nation. Or perhaps—the Justice Department willing—you would like to obtain 95 percent of the market for your product lines.

It is not important that you never attain this goal. In fact, if you do attain it, it was probably not far out enough to constitute a true dream goal. But having a dream goal gives you something to reach for, and, though you will never succeed in attaining it, you cannot help but improve your performance. As one crack-er-barrel philosopher once observed, "If you continually reach for a star, you may never actually get it but the chances of dragging your feet in the mud will be considerably less."

In my own case, I had a youthful dream goal to be the President of the United States. As I matured, the idea of being President changed from a dream goal to something you couldn't sell me for all the gold in Fort Knox. But I believe that having that early dream goal was at least partially responsible for whatever success I have had.

Let us assume that you have established a goal for the current year, a goal for the next five or ten years, and a dream goal. You are convinced that these goals are worthwhile and—in the case of all but the dream goal—largely attainable. You are not yet through, however! You must now convince your team that these goals are worthwhile and attainable, for if they don't come to be "believers" you are never going to reach your goals.

Have you ever come home full of good intentions and said to your wife, "You're working too hard and I'm taking you to Paris as soon as we can save the money"? Now, the dear little lady might like nothing better than a trip to Paris, but chances are she's going to throw cold water all over your good intentions. You may have thought going to Paris was a marvelous goal, but you didn't convince her that it was attainable and worthwhile—and, more important, you didn't consult her before making a final decision.

The point here is that very few goals are so utterly perfect in their conception that others will accept them without question and indeed nominate you for the Nobel Prize in goal setting. And even if such perfection could be achieved, the goal is unlikely to be accepted automatically by others simply because they didn't think of it themselves. People—and your team members are no exception—like to be convinced that a goal is worthwhile and attainable, and they like to be able to put in their two cents' worth. (And, although it is difficult for us to admit it, their two cents' worth sometimes amounts to a dollar!)

You should therefore assemble the members of your team, present to them your goal and the rationale behind it, and invite their comments and reactions. Such a discussion will probably not be totally efficient in its results, and you must expect to receive a lot of chaff (and gaff) with the wheat. Your sales manager, if he is like most sales managers, will probably tell you that your goal is too low, for sales managers seem to be incurable optimists. On the other hand, your manufacturing manager will wring his hands and give you a thousand reasons why the goal can never be met, for manufacturing managers seem to be uniformly pessimistic.

The importance of this group meeting, however, lies not so much in the quality of the ideas and inputs you receive (although these can be very important), but in the fact that each of your subordinates has been given a chance to contribute to something of vital importance to the whole team. You have shown them implicitly that their ideas are important to you. And even though the group may never fully agree on the course of action to be taken and you have to make the final decision yourself, you have very subtly turned "your" goal into "our" goal. It is only when your team introjects the goal into their own personal motivation mechanisms that it has a real chance of accomplishment.

To summarize, not only do you have to know where you are going, but your team has to believe that you know where you are going.

Let us assume that you have followed the steps just mentioned. You have set your goal and you have convinced your team that it is worthwhile and attainable. You are still not through, however. You must have a *plan* to reach the goal.

Suppose you and your team have agreed that the goal for this year is to manufacture and market a million pairs of roller skates. You can't end the goal-setting process at that point with an inspirational exhortation such as, "O.K., boys, let's get out and make it!" You must have a definite plan to manufacture and sell those roller skates. The plan may include the addition of new plant facilities, the training of new supervisory personnel, an increase in the sales staff, new advertising and promotional materials, or whatever.

It was only a few years ago that Roger Bannister made the history books by being the first man to run a mile in under four minutes. In accomplishing this feat, Bannister had a goal, but he also had a plan for attaining that goal. He didn't decide merely to start running as fast as he could once the gun went off, hoping that, if he didn't collapse halfway through the race, he would finish the mile in under four minutes. He had a plan for the race. He decided that, if he was going to make his goal, he would have to run the first quarter-mile in, say, 59 seconds. He also concluded that he would have to reach the halfway point in, say, 2:03 or 2:04 and the three-quarter mark in, say, 3:01. The next thing that Bannister did was form a team to help him attain the goal. Three men, armed with stop watches, stood at the quarter-mile positions and advised him of the time he had taken to reach their respective points. As he went along, Bannister compared his actual progress with his plan and made compensating adjustments, until one day he reached his goal. He never would have made it, however, without his precise plan.

Plans should be written if they are to succeed. To put it another way, if you can't put your plan in writing, you don't have a plan. I have found that the act of writing out a plan invariably leads to the creation of a better plan. Cold print seems to expose fallacies, voids, and inconsistencies better than any other method.

Nowadays, if the word "planning" is mentioned to many managers, their first thought is to go out and hire a long-range planner and then get back to more important things. I have nothing against long-range planners, and in fact I think that, properly utilized, they can be of valuable assistance to management. It is important to remember, however, that they are aids to, not substitutes for, good management.

In discussing long-range planning, let us first consider what is meant by the term. Many executives think that long-range planning has something to do with what will happen in the next fiscal year. To them, five- and ten-year plans are "super" long-range planning.

I consider five- and ten-year plans not to be long-range planning at all. They are merely intermediate-term plans. To me, long-range planning is the consideration of what businesses the company is now in and should be in and the formulation of broad objectives to take the company in the right direction over the next 20 or 30 years. As an example, I suspect that the railroad executives of the early 1900's never took the time to ask themselves, "What is our business?" I am sure that they instinctively assumed that their business was railroading. Yet, if they had taken the time to ask themselves this question, they might have concluded that they were really in the business of transporting men and materials from one place to another. Had these railroad executives gone through this truly long-range planning process, the railroad industry might not be having the problems it is experiencing today. At the very least, the industry wouldn't have been caught napping when trucks and airplanes came on the scene.

Once having determined what business the company is really in, the manager must then ask himself, "Is this a good business to be in? Has it got a future?" A corollary question to ask is, "If we weren't in our present business and had nothing but cash, would we go into this business?" Seeking the answers to these very broad questions is what I mean by long-range planning.

Long-range planning of this type is a job that a manager cannot delegate to his long-range planner. The latter is of great use in providing analyses and projections to aid the manager's thinking, but ultimately it is the manager who does his own long-range planning.

Long-range planning is not something that can be accomplished on one's lunch hour or in between appointments. I have found it a very desirable technique to get away from it all and go to the mountains (often with my team) or anywhere far removed from the office. It is in this sort of environment that one can think and dream. A number of progressive companies also employ this process. For example, the whole top management team of a certain company goes to a farm in Vermont once a year and sits under the trees discussing in a very informal and unstructured way the directions the company should be taking—not next year, but many years hence. Management critics have often dismissed such retreats as a form of boondoggling—the expense-paid vacation. I believe that they miss the point completely, for a manager with many daily problems and "fire drills" simply cannot spend the time he needs to think intelligently about the future unless he can isolate himself for a while. It is not accidental, I believe, that church retreats, in this age of rapid communication and tremendous technology, are becoming more popular than ever.

Although I have termed five- and ten-year plans as something less than long-range planning, this is not to imply that they are not extremely useful in keeping the company on the track over the near term. I am more than a little dismayed, however, at the amount of utterly worthless junk that comes under the heading of a "five-year plan." Some company presidents have proudly shown me their five-year plans as an example of twentieth century enlightened management. On examination, these plans are nothing more than simple extrapolations of the increases that occurred this year over last year. For example, sales went up 10 percent this year, so the five-year plan assumes that sales will go up precisely 10 percent for each of the next five years. And the same with manufacturing costs, number of employees, and profit.

Such a plan is no plan at all. It is merely window dressing.

A properly executed five-year plan should answer questions such as—

- What products are becoming obsolete and should be either retreaded or discontinued?
- What new products are coming out of the research

laboratories, and what sort of volume can be expected of them?

- What technological challenges are going to be hurled at us by our competitors, and how do we meet them?
- What sort of capital spending is needed to improve efficiency and meet the projected sales volumes?
- What are the expected trends in compensation costs for executives, middle managers, foremen, engineers, hourly production workers?
- What sorts of new manpower skills must the company have, and in what quantities?
- What is likely to be the national and regional economic climate?

These are not intended to comprise an exhaustive list of items that should be considered as part of a five-year plan. Answering questions of this type, however, will insure that the plan is a meaningful blueprint for the future and not merely an arithmetic extension of the past.

What are the types of goals you should establish for your organization? Sales and profits, of course, come immediately to mind. Other important goals are return on sales, capital expenditures, manufacturing costs, sales costs, inventory-to-sales ratios, advertising plans, and research and development expenditures (and the products that will emerge therefrom).

The single most important goal in my opinion, however, is return on the investment of your stockholders. They have put up the capital to run your business when they could easily have invested it in any number of other enterprises. Every business action should be taken with a view to maximizing the return to the stockholders over the long term.

I have been confounded a number of times by presidents of companies who brag about their raw profit dollars or about their return on sales. To me, a 16 percent after-tax return on sales is utterly without value if that profit represents only a 3 percent return on the investment of the company's stockholders. In this instance, the stockholders could more profitably have invested their funds in government bonds and received complete protection of principal to boot.

Another goal that many companies stress is cost reduction. This is an admirable objective in any business, but it is usually couched in a rather narrow way. The very term "cost reduction" implies that current costs should be reduced. The real meaning, of cost reduction, however, is to reduce costs *relative to sales*, even though costs next year are 25 percent higher in absolute dollars than they were this year. From this standpoint, truly effective cost reduction may warrant the expenditure of considerable sums of money. For example, thousands may be spent on a number of labor-saving machines which, even after considering the additional capital involved, substantially reduce the unit costs of manufacturing and provide an excellent return to the stockholders. Yet many managers, entranced by the words "cost reduction," would never think to spend money in order to save money.

In my experience, I have tried to avoid using the words "cost reduction" because of their narrow implication. Instead, I use the words "profit improvement." These convey the ultimate goal of any cost-reduction program and make it possible to think positively and expansively.

III

Organization

As a manager, you have established your goals and your plans for accomplishing them. You must now organize a team to get the work done.

Before proceeding, let us consider just what an organization is. Broadly defined, *an organization is a group of people working together toward a common goal under a single leadership.* Viewed in this manner, not one but many organizations exist within a single company. A group of production workers combine to form an organization under one foreman, and this team works toward a specific goal in its production subdepartment. A group of foremen combine to form an organization under one superintendent, and this team works toward a larger goal. And so on, right up to the president.

Each of the many organizations within a company has a single leader. But not only does this individual lead his team; he is also a member of a higher team. This dual role of managerial personnel extends even to the president, who leads a team consisting of his vice-presidents and key staff members; and he is a member of another and higher team—the board of directors.

Dedicated sports fans spend endless time developing their personal "team of the century." In their minds they assemble a superteam—men of the quality of Frankie Albert, Y. A. Tittle, Joe Namath, O. J. Simpson, and so on. To them, such a combination of superstars would literally be unbeatable.

Acting on these fantasies, sports promoters have regularly formed two such superteams and pitted them against each other. The result has usually been something of a disappointment. Often, such a motley collection of allstars is easy prey for a well-coached but second-rate team that played together regularly.

The second-rate team probably has nothing even remotely resembling an allstar on it, but what it does have is *organization*. Each member of that team knows what he is supposed to do when a certain play is called. More important, he knows what every other member of the team is supposed to do. The allstars, on the other hand, practice together for only a few hours before the game. About the most they can do is learn the moves they personally are to make in a certain play. Learning the moves of all the other players is a luxury they do not have the time for. It is a tribute to the individual playing ability of these superstars that they don't run into each other on every play!

A business team is really not much different from a football team. And, like a football team, it will be effective only when every man on the team knows—

- What the goal is.
- What part he is to play in attaining the goal.
- What part each of the other team members is going to play in the attainment of the goal.
- What part you, the leader, are going to play in the attainment of the goal. (This requirement is unique to a business organization.)

Only when these conditions are fulfilled will the management team be an effective force.

To accomplish these organizational fundamentals requires organization charts and position descriptions.

An organization chart is needed to delineate the leader and the members of each management team. In certain companies which do not publish organization charts, some individuals are actually unsure as to just who their boss really is or who else is supposed to be on their team working alongside them.

Written position descriptions are also required if the organization is to function properly. Unfortunately, the art of preparing a meaningful and useful position description is rather hard to master. Phrases like "Coordinates financial management" and "Participates in production planning activities" are absolutely meaningless because they don't tell the incumbent—or his fellow team members—precisely what he is supposed to do.

I believe that position descriptions should be oriented to the decisions or major recommendations an individual is required to make. Statements like "Has final approval authority on all capital expenditures of $100,000 or less" or "Approves company bargaining positions and wage settlements" are meaningful because they delineate the lines of responsibility in a given position and tell both the incumbent and his team members just what that individual can and can't do.

Although not too many professionals in management may agree with me, I believe that the individual's goals for the year should also be incorporated within his position description. For example, I would expand the regular position description of my sales manager to include such objectives as—

- Your specific goal this year is to sell a million pairs of roller skates.
- To do this, you are being given a budget of $126,500 for expenses other than salaries and $100,000 for salaries.
- You are to set the price on roller skates for this year, after consulting with and receiving inputs from the manufacturing and financial managers.
- You are to have seven salesmen this year to accomplish the stated objectives.

32

In a sense, the regular position description represents somewhat of a generic description of the individual's basic and ongoing responsibilities. The incorporation of annual goals into the incumbent's basic position description fleshes it out and transforms it into a specific description of the position for this particular year.

Valid, written position descriptions are as vital to the successful management of a company as musical scores are to the successful performance of an orchestra. In my view, a symphony orchestra is a good example in microcosm of how to organize a management team.

- Its members have a common goal: to play beautiful music.
- It has a single leader: the conductor.
- It has written position descriptions in the form of musical scores. These tell each player what to play and when.

Can you imagine an orchestra where the players are not quite sure who the leader is? Or one where each player is free to play any note he desires at any time he chooses? The result would be sheer chaos and certainly not very pleasing to the ear.

Yet that is the direction in which some companies seem to be heading. These companies often point with pride to the fact that they have no organization charts and no position descriptions. They feel that these are nothing more than stultifying constraints which can only impede individual initiative and creativity. Some company presidents who operate in this manner believe that not telling their vice-presidents just what it is they are supposed to do will make the best of them take on added responsibilities without being told, and eventually the next president will emerge triumphant from the pack. Such an approach is what I would term the "Darwinian theory of organization." It invites a power struggle and usually creates an atmosphere reminiscent of the court of the Borgias in its prime. Although I have yet to meet anyone who will admit it, I feel that this approach is used by some presidents, consciously or unconsciously, to consolidate their own power and entrench themselves in their positions through a divide-and-conquer strategy through the generation of a great deal of insecurity in their team members.

A consequence of not establishing written position descriptions is that some tasks are overdone and some are not done at all. When I first came to one company, I inadvertently discovered that determining the amount and type of products that went into the warehouse was no one person's responsibility. The manufacturing manager kept turning out the products, and he thought the sales manager was controlling the inventory. The sales manager—like most sales managers—was concerned only with selling the product. As far as he was concerned, the more inventory there was, the less likely he was to run out of stock. The controller wasn't responsible either, and, since the company was making money, he wasn't inclined to ask questions.

Had the previous management taken the time to prepare written position descriptions, it would have become obvious fairly quickly that no one had been assigned responsibility to control the levels of inventory in the warehouse. That same set of position descriptions might also have revealed that two or even three people had been assigned the responsibility for some other task.

A question that always arises in any discussion of management organization is the proper number of people who should report to one manager. In my view, there is no single span-of-control figure that is optimum for every situation. The biggest variable affecting span of control is the type of organization that is being utilized. If the organization is highly centralized, it is likely that the manager can handle at most only six or seven line subordinates plus a small number of staff personnel.

On the other hand, if the organization is highly decentralized, with many autonomous profit centers, a top executive can probably handle a very large number of subordinates since, by definition, none of these individuals is going to require much supervision. I have seen some decentralized organizations where a general manager has as many as 25 profit center managers reporting to him and is quite able to cope with a span of control of these dimensions.

Another subject of interest here is the formation of committees. The committee-breeding capacity of some companies approaches that of rabbits. In those companies, people are continually heard to remark, "Well, let's refer that to the X committee for decision."

I think that committees, when properly used, can be valuable management tools. But committees should not be decision-making bodies; they should be used only as information-gathering and information-dispensing devices. Any company that lets a majority vote of a committee decide whether to build a new plant in Keokuk is making a potentially costly mistake. A committee should be assembled and told that an expansion in production capacity is needed. It should be told of the various sites under consideration and the advantages and disadvantages of each. At that point, each committee member should have the chance to comment on the desirability or undesirability of each site from his particular point of view. For example, the sales manager might prefer to have the plant in Chicago, since that is where his largest territory is located. The production manager might like Keokuk because it is near a convenient source of raw materials and has excellent transportation facilities. The personnel manager might like a third city because he just learned that another company is planning to put a very large plant in Keokuk which would probably drain off the labor supply.

In this example, the committee is being used as it should: as a means of communicating various points of view among the team members and to the team leader. Ultimately, however, the person responsible for that new plant is going to have to make the final decision, using the inputs supplied by the committee. I suspect that even in companies famous for their numerous committees, some one executive really makes the final decision.

Of course, committees which *do* make actual decisions on a majority vote basis have one thing going for them. They permit responsibility to be shared so that, if something blows up, no one executive can be fingered as the culprit. Of course a company must often pay the price for this comforting avoidance of responsibility in rather ponderous decision making. As a result, the company finds itself outdistanced by competitors whose executives are willing to grab the ball and run with it. When that happens, the committee members who banded together for comfort and avoidance of responsibility can take added comfort from the fact that they will probably all be fired together.

IV

Decentralization and Delegation

I t is interesting to witness the maturation and growth of a small company. At first the president makes every decision himself. He signs all the purchase orders, even those for paper clips. He approves every salary increase, even for the janitor. He goes out on all major sales calls with his sales manager to be sure that nothing goes wrong.

Time passes and the company grows. The president works harder and harder. Signing the purchase orders now takes three hours a day, not to mention the salary increases and the sales calls. If the president ever gets a free moment, and is at all a perceptive type, he will begin to wonder where all this is taking him. Eventually, he reasons, either he will have to let others make some decisions or he is likely to end up with an ulcer, followed rather speedily by his first—and maybe his last—coronary.

If the president decides to delegate some of his responsibilities, he is moving with—not against—the laws of evolution, because the presidents who don't delegate all die out very quickly.

At first, delegation is a haphazard thing, but eventually our president gets the hang of it and begins to adopt one of the most important management fundamentals: true decentralization.

In my early business career, I used to think decentralization meant that a president should put one of his plants in Los Angeles, another in Chicago, and a third in New York. And if he *really* believed in decentralization, a fourth plant in London was just the thing!

I soon learned that what I meant by "decentralization" was in reality "dispersion."

What, then, is decentralization? It is *the delegation of authority and responsibility down the line in your organization to the point where every decision is made at the lowest possible level where that particular decision can be made intelligently.*

What is the "lowest possible level"? It is the level where all the information necessary to make the decision and all the skills and experience necessary to evaluate the information combine.

Decentralization is therefore a management concept, not a mechanical dispersion of assets. The two can be combined quite effectively, however, for I have found that, having once delegated responsibility, it is easier to avoid interfering in a subordinate's decisions if he is 2,000 miles away rather than right down the hall.

Decentralization, in the proper sense of the word, doesn't just happen. To accomplish it properly requires a considerable amount of planning. The first step is for the potential delegator to sit down and write his own position description, listing every one of his current duties and responsibilities and all the decisions he makes. The next step is to consider which of these responsibilities and decisions can be given to someone else—anyone else. Obviously the least important decisions are the first to go. Why, for example, should the executive sign every purchase order? Why not sign only those where the expenditure exceeds $100,000?

Having rid oneself of the less important decisions, one should then consider which decisions are so important as to absolutely prohibit their delegation. These should of course be retained, but almost all of the middle group of decisions—those neither of vital importance nor of relatively little importance—can probably be delegated also.

Next, our potential delegator must consider to whom he is going to assign the decisions he is delegating. Many of these decisions will find a proper home simply on the basis of disciplinary criteria. That is to say, the manufacturing decisions go to the manufacturing manager; the personnel decisions go to the personnel manager. These decisions, in other words, are given to people who have the requisite skills and experience to make them.

But these people may not necessarily have all the information necessary to make them. Accordingly, the delegator may have to create systems to provide the new decision makers with the information they need.

The last step in the delegation process is to rewrite the position descriptions of those who are about to take on added decision-making responsibilities and to inform these individuals of their new roles.

Decentralization, as I have described it, may sound deceptively simple, but it isn't. Two basic behavioral problems are often exhibited in the delegation process:

1. The subordinate may resist his new responsibility.
2. The delegator may secretly want to keep his current responsibility.

It often happens that a subordinate to whom you have delegated a decision comes back to you and says, "Boss, I'm faced with several alternatives. Which do you think is the best?" Now, it is a natural temptation for a manager to preen his feathers and, speaking *ex cathedra*, deliver a sonorous discourse on the alternative that should be taken. The end result, however, is that he, and not his subordinate, made the decision.

What should a manager do when confronted with this situation? Refuse to speak to his subordinate? Of course not! I have found it useful to play the role of a sounding board, asking questions such as, "Have you considered the ramifications of this aspect of your decision? Do you think the disadvantages of this decision outweigh its advantages?" Quite often the subordinate talks himself into a decision. But sometimes there is no alternative but for me to offer my opinion. This I will do when I have no choice. But I have always told my subordinates, "I'll give you my opinion, but it is only just that. You know more about this than I do, and you must make the decision yourself. If you follow my opinion, that makes you no less responsible for the decision because, if it is wrong, you will be to blame for relying on such obviously stupid counsel."

The reverse of the coin in delegation is interfering in decisions that are about to be made by your subordinates. I have had a number of presidents ask me incredulously, "You mean you would let a subordinate make a decision, even if you knew it was wrong?" Well, let's analyze that question a moment. Its key words are, "even if you knew it was wrong." But how does a man know a decision is wrong? Just because he would have made a different decision doesn't necessarily imply that his subordinate is taking an incorrect course of action.

Usually, this type of interference stems from the fact that the manager held his subordinate's job before he got promoted. Of course, in his mind, that makes him the world's greatest authority on that position; after all, he wouldn't have been promoted if that were not true. It is no doubt correct that on the day he was promoted, he knew more than his successor. But remember that as each day passes, he knows less and less about that position and his subordinate knows more and more. It doesn't take too long before his subordinate knows more about that job than he does—or ever did.

So, if you as a manager ever feel like shooting off your mouth to your subordinate, telling him, "I remember trying that idea ten years ago and it flopped miserably," consider for a moment that your subordinate will probably be thinking, "Sure, boss, it's no wonder it flopped, considering who was running the department!"

This is not to imply, however, that you must never under any circumstances interfere in the decisions of your subordinates. If you sincerely believe that a decision would put the organization into a severe crisis, then you would be derelict in your duty if you did not intervene. But a "severe crisis" means just that and does not extend to decisions which, in your less and less informed opinion, are merely likely to cost the organization a little money.

I might also add that the fact that a subordinate falls flat on his face as a result of a minor decision is often worth much more over the long run than the loss of a few dollars. For we seem to learn more from our mistakes than from our successes. To one degree or another, all of us "adults" are still pretty childish. We can be given all the best advice, but sooner or later we are going to have to try it our way, if for no other reason than to satisfy ourselves that it really is the wrong thing to do. I can remember repeatedly warning my small children not to touch the radiator. Of course, they insisted in disregarding my advice, until I reached the point of telling them "O.K., touch it—you'll learn!" Learn they did, and very fast, too.

True decentralization imposes one other requirement on a manager. He must deal only with his own team members. Again, I have had presidents ask me incredulously, "You mean I—the top man—cannot go anywhere I want in my organization and say anything I want?" Well, he *can* go anywhere he wants, but he had better be very careful as to what he says, or he will end up interfering in the decisions of other managers who aren't even members of his own team.

Take the case of Mr. A, the company president, who finds himself in Keokuk one day with some time on his hands. His company has a plant in Keokuk, but that is not why Mr. A is there. In fact, Mr. A was born in Keokuk, his aged mother still lives there, and he started his career in the plant, working his way up to plant manager and eventually to the presidency of the company. Mr. A flew in over the weekend to visit his ailing mother, but he was unable to leave on Monday morning because the airport was fogged in. So, having some time on his hands, Mr. A decides to visit his old plant. He walks in and introduces himself to the plant manager, whom he has never met. After the initial obeisance has been received and the plant manager has recovered from the shock, Mr. A says, "I didn't come here for any specific purpose; I used to work here 30 years ago and would enjoy seeing the old plant again, so you just go about your work and I'll wander through the plant." Well, of course, the plant manager is obviously less than ecstatic about turning the president loose in his plant, but what can he do? So into the plant goes Mr. A, and a few feet later, whom should he encounter but old Joe, who used to work on the bench alongside Mr. A 30 years ago and is still at it.

Naturally, Mr. A can't resist the temptation to go up to old Joe and clap him on the back. The two exchange some reminiscences, and then the president says, "How are things going, Joe?" Well, that's where Mr. A made his first mistake. Joe replies, "I guess things in general are going all right, but that new plant manager you got here is a real dog." Mr. A answers in a confidential tone, "Well, we're aware of some of the problems in this plant, Joe, and it won't be long before we do something about it."

That was Mr. A's second—and gravest—mistake. In one sentence, he undercut the plant manager, the district superintendent, and the vice-president of manufacturing. He went several levels down in the organization and interfered in a decision that had been delegated to someone else. And in the process he wreaked a good deal of havoc which will not be easily undone.

The ultimate in decentralization is the delegation of

45

profit and loss responsibility to a subordinate. Now, the term "profit and loss responsibility" is bandied about rather loosely in industry these days. I have seen many so-called division managers who have been assigned profit and loss responsibility for their products, but who controlled neither the engineering nor the manufacture of those products. In effect, such people are glorified sales managers, and to assign them profit and loss responsibility is at best a travesty and can at worst result in considerable harm to the organization.

In my view, it is not possible to have true profit and loss responsibility unless the functions of sales, manufacturing, and product engineering report to one manager. If he has staff functions under him as well, such as personnel, finance, legal, and so on, so much the better. The absence of these staff functions, however, does not prevent delegation of true profit and loss responsibility to the manager as long as he has sales, manufacturing, and engineering.

Another requirement of true profit and loss decentralization is the establishment of fair transfer pricing policies between divisions. It often occurs that one division buys a good deal of its raw materials or semifinished products from another division. A continual problem is determining what price the buying division is going to pay its sister selling division. To the extent that these transfer prices are established arbitrarily or capriciously, no true profit and loss responsibility in either division can be said to exist.

Some companies have sought to solve the transfer pricing problem by authorizing the buying division to purchase on the outside if it can obtain a better deal. Of course, a prudent division manager is not likely to take such a course of action unless he has an absolutely ironclad case. Nevertheless, the threat of outside procurement and the established concept that transfer prices should be set with reference to competitive levels help to bring recalcitrant selling divisions into line and allow true profit and loss responsibility to be assigned.

In my experience, I have found it desirable to require that a selling division sell at a slight discount from the going rate when the sale is to a sister division. My reasoning is that the selling division has fewer selling costs than it would have if the sale were made to an outside party. Obviously, the selling division doesn't have to advertise its products, and its direct selling expenses are comparably lower as well. Such an approach gives the selling division the same profit it would have received on the outside after deducting its selling expenses, and it gives the buying division a slight price break and therefore a tangible incentive to do business within the company.

V

Selecting Your Team

*T*his chapter covers the selection of managers for your team. As such, it is concerned with internal selection, including promotion; external selection of individuals from other companies; and the selection of whole management teams from the outside through the acquisition process.

To me, there is only one management fundamental concerning selection, and it is so deceptively simple that very few people think of it and many violate it. The rule: *If the man is going to work directly for you, you select him.*

Now, it is obvious that you as a busy manager cannot take the time to screen a million people in order to pick the one person who is right for your organization. You must have professional help—people to advertise for candidates, people to test the candidates, people to handle the initial assessment of their capabilities. But sooner or later there are only five or six left of the many who originally applied for the job. This is where you come in.

You must interview these finalists yourself; you must assess their backgrounds and their strong and weak points; you must hear the reactions of the professional selection experts and the psychologists; and you must ultimately make the final decision as to who gets the job. There is no shortcut to this aspect of the selection process. This is a job you cannot and must not delegate to someone else in your organization.

To underscore this simple fundamental of selection, I have in speeches contrasted it with some pretty far-out examples of selection "applications." For example, when I was lecturing in Europe some time ago, I told my audience, "You can use phrenology, for all I care, and analyze the bumps on your candidates' heads to your heart's content. But the main thing is to make the ultimate selection decision yourself." I thought that the use of phrenology—which is about as far out as you can get—served as a vivid contrast to the point I was trying to make. But no sooner was the lecture finished than three personnel people in the audience came up to tell me that phrenology was the technique they were using! So, when I moved to England to continue my lecture series, I switched examples and this time told my audience, "You can use graphology for all I care, and analyze the handwriting of your candidates, but the main thing is to make the ultimate selection decision yourself." This time twelve personnel people in the audience came up to tell me that graphology was the technique they were using!

As a result of these two experiences, I no longer consider any far-out examples safe, so I can only repeat that it doesn't matter a great deal what selection techniques you use as long as you, the manager, interview the finalists and make the final selection yourself.

In the chapter on delegation, we discussed the proclivity of many managers to interfere in the decisions of their subordinates and the proclivity of many subordinates to try and get their managers to make all the decisions. These tendencies exist in the selection area as well.

It will often happen that one of your direct subordinates has an opening on his team. Of course, you have the perfect candidate in mind; he may be your nephew or someone you have observed from afar in the organization. It is a terrible temptation to call your subordinate into your office and say, "If I were you, I'd hire John." The translation of this statement reads, "You had damn well better hire John." At any rate, most perceptive subordinates get the message, and, by a not so fortuitous turn of events, John gets the job. In the process, however, you have violated a management fundamental by interfering in a prime management decision of your subordinate. You have caused him to hire someone who may not have been the person he would have hired had he had a completely free hand. When you come right down to it, if you as a manager can't pick your personal team with complete autonomy, you really have no autonomy at all and can't be held responsible for the actions of your group.

Now, this is not to say that you can't use a subtle amount of influence if you have a candidate in mind for a job on your subordinate's team. You can always work through the personnel department and slip your man in above the "screen" so that he ends up as one of the five or six finalists. But if you are playing the game right you mustn't tell your subordinate what you have done; if he inadvertently rejects your candidate, so be it.

In other situations, your subordinate will come to you and ask you to interview a candidate he is considering. On the surface this appears to be a perfectly reasonable request, but I have often wondered whether it actually is a means whereby your subordinate can dodge his decision-making responsibility. If you interview the man and conclude he is great, and your subordinate hires him, you are ultimately responsible if that man doesn't work out. Personally, I am inclined to refuse to interview any candidates for any positions except those which are part of my own management team. I firmly believe that the team leader should be the ultimate decision maker when it comes to selecting members of his team. If I believe that my subordinate can't be trusted in this highly fundamental and personal area, then I am a person who can't delegate or my subordinate is not to be trusted in any area of management decision making and should be removed.

At the heart of the selection process, I believe, is the need for a sort of personal chemistry between the manager and his potential subordinate. The personnel department can use psychological tests, phrenology, graphology, or whatever, but if there is no immediate rapport between these two people, the probability is that the combination will not work out over the long run.

I am amused by the mismatches that are caused by violating the principle that a manager should select his own people. One instance I recall concerned a highly aggressive manager who, when questioned by the psychological selection consultants as to what sort of subordinate he wanted, replied, "I want a real go-getter; a man who is not afraid to challenge his boss and speak up; one, preferably, who is or will shortly be better than his boss." Now, this description could only fit Jack Armstrong. It sketched out the type of individual that any red-blooded manager would crawl over broken glass on his belly to obtain. In this instance, however, it was a complete fabrication. The aggressive manager I am thinking about would have been appalled to have such a self-starter in his organization. What he really wanted, but was afraid to request, was a Caspar Milquetoast type who would sit at his feet all day and applaud his every action.

The point to be made here is that there is no one ideal all-purpose subordinate to fit every manager. It takes all types, and none of them is necessarily wrong. That is why the selection process must be an intimate one. After all, you wouldn't allow someone to select a wife for you. Why, then, should you allow someone else to select a subordinate for you—someone with whom you must of necessity forge a close relationship?

Selecting managers is an especially difficult task. Time after time, I have seen the best salesman picked to be the sales manager or the best engineer picked to be the engineering manager. If the best salesman actually does turn out to be a good sales manager, it is usually an unadulterated coincidence, unless the salesman just happens to be a good manager of his time, his budget, his territory—his life.

Regrettably, there often seems to be a negative correlation between good technical talent and good managerial talent. It frequently happens that the magnificent engineer who is rewarded for his accomplishments by being promoted to manager enters his plush new office and, when no one is looking, pulls down the shades and plays with his slide rule. The last thing he wants to do is spend his time telling a bunch of mere mortals how to be engineers. He wants to be back on the boards, working at the state of the art, for that is where he gets his kicks.

The same is often true of the outstanding salesman who is promoted to sales manager. The idea of sitting behind a desk filling out reports for the home office is anathema to him. What he wants is to get out and sell face to face.

I was interested to note that one very large company took the time to study the backgrounds of its successful engineering supervisors. Almost to a man, this company found, the best engineering supervisors graduated in the lower half of their classes and had made no distinguishing marks as engineers. In fact, these successful engineering supervisors by and large detested pure engineering. What they wanted to do was manage, and, given the chance, they were outstanding.

The fact is, people generally enjoy doing what they do well. If a man is a superb engineer or salesman, why would he enjoy doing something totally different? Since management is a discipline unto itself and is totally different from selling or engineering, it is unlikely that many top flight salesmen or engineers will really want to become managers. They have found success—the psychologists call it "closure"—in their current professions.

Very few things are black or white in business, but if I have a choice between a good salesman or engineer, and a good manager, I would certainly choose the manager, even if he knew nothing about sales or engineering. In the latter case, the individual will learn the basic technical aspects of the field in a very short time and then go on to become an excellent sales or engineering manager. On the other hand, the unfortunate soul who is the world's best salesman or engineer, but who knows little or nothing about managing, will have the department in chaos within a few weeks.

I have seen many companies needlessly go to the outside for talent when they had ample talent within their own company but didn't know it. This is unfortunate not only for the company but for the individual. I recall that one of my acquaintances started his career with a giant retailing chain. He reasoned that promotion was a combination of skill and being in the right place at the right time. Since the company he chose was so big, and promotional opportunities were occurring daily, he believed that he could eliminate the "luck" factor and would be promoted just as soon as he demonstrated the necessary skills. What he didn't know, however, was that this company very seldom transferred a manager from one territory to another. In fact, it was the rare manager who was moved from one store to another. This giant retailer turned out not to be a giant at all; rather, it was a collection of a thousand individual stores.

How does a large corporation assure that it is not overlooking valuable in-house personnel? One answer, I believe, is to establish an inventory of management talent. Vital statistics on each current and potential manager are kept in a centralized location. These include such things as educational background, experience, performance ratings, geographical preferences, and the like. When openings arise anywhere in the organization above a certain level, these must be reported to the centralized location. The names of any qualified candidates are drawn from the inventory and sent to the unit making the selection.

Now, many companies have established these so-called skills inventories, investing countless thousands of dollars in the process, and yet very few of them have worked. What usually happens is that the manager making the selection already knows whom he wants, for, more than likely, the individual is currently working in a lower position in his department. So he rejects the carefully gleaned résumés sent to him by the corporate staff. It is difficult to combat this problem, but I would suggest that one solution is to make the manager who is doing the selecting interview each and every qualified candidate from within the company. He may still pick the "known quantity"; but, if he is exposed to other qualified individuals on a face-to-face basis, there is always the chance that he may find someone better.

Many managers spend hours contemplating the capital expenditures they are going to make in the next year—and even over the next five years. Yet these same managers often fail miserably in planning for their management manpower needs during the same period of time. While the company president is telling a Waldorf Astoria audience that "my people are my most important asset," many of his subordinates are acting as though people were neither important nor an asset.

Only in the highly service-oriented industries which utilize rare types of talents have I found a pragmatic awareness of the importance of good people. I remember one president of a large advertising agency who remarked, "95 percent of my inventory goes down in the elevator every night." Executives in these types of businesses have very little in the way of physical assets. They have their noses rubbed daily in the fact that only one thing makes them better than their competitors: the caliber of their people. This is generally true of industrial firms also—at least over the long run—but when one has shiny mills and electronic equipment to show off, it becomes more than a little obscured.

I believe a company must do just as good a job of manpower planning as it does in capital budgeting and market planning. More than once, I have seen a president react with utter surprise when confronted with the retirement of a key subordinate. Such a reaction is inexcusable, for retirement, like death and taxes, is a certainty.

I think that twice a year a company should prepare a chart showing all its top and middle management positions, along with the ages and performance ratings of the incumbents. A cursory analysis of this chart will show the retirements that are going to occur over the next few years. Certain other executives may have to be replaced because of poor performance. New positions may open up because of organizational expansion, and these have to be considered also. The end result of this inspection will be a good idea of the vacancies that are likely to occur within the time under consideration.

Armed with this knowledge, your next step is to consider who is going to fill these vacancies. Perhaps there is one individual (maybe even two) who is ready to be promoted. He can then be listed against the expected vacancy. Perhaps there is no one ready to fill the opening, but one individual could be ready in a year if given the right type of development. One value of this manpower planning exercise is in uncovering this fact and setting in motion the development activities that will enable this individual to be ready at the proper time to assume the position.

When this replacement planning process is carried down through the organization, it is then possible to determine how many executives will have to be hired from the outside and how many management trainees will have to be started at the bottom of the organization to insure adequate staffing in the future.

Many things can happen to upset these carefully laid manpower plans. On occasion a capable executive will be so inconsiderate as to die before retirement age—or, worse yet—to quit and join a competitor. Or the bright young man you were planning to develop turns out not to be as bright as you thought he was. These various imponderables make it mandatory, as I mentioned earlier, for manpower planning to be carried out at least twice a year. The fact that these unforeseen events occur, however, is no excuse for failing to try to do the very best possible job of manpower planning, for the fallout effects of looking at the company's management manpower needs overshadow the revisions that have to be made.

A selection policy used by some companies is to promote exclusively from within the organization. On its face, such a policy is very appealing to those already inside the company, because it guarantees that all the competition they are ever going to have is right around them.

In my experience, however, promotion exclusively from within can be a dangerous course of action. I certainly agree that whenever a logical candidate can be found within the organization, he should have first crack at a promotional opportunity. But it often happens that there really is no logical candidate ready for the higher job. In that case, I favor going outside and hiring the best man I can find.

The Egyptian pharaohs (and, more recently, hemophiliac descendants of Queen Victoria) discovered that inbreeding accentuates all the positive hereditary traits, but, unfortunately, the negative ones as well. I think this is also true of business organizations. An injection of new blood can have startling effects, and I am in favor of it. I think that as a matter of policy about 10 to 15 percent of executive vacancies should be filled from the outside. Not only does this approach bring in new talent; it also tends to keep the current and would-be executives within the company on their toes.

There are many techniques for hiring a man from the outside, but I personally prefer using an executive search firm. The high compensation that these recruiters earn helps to insure that they are the cream of the crop among selection professionals. In addition, they have a more objective viewpoint than inside selection personnel.

However, good results are obtained from an executive searcher only if he is used intelligently. By this I mean that you must spend the time with the searcher to detail the duties and responsibilities of the position; what you are like; and precisely what sort of man you want. This means being totally honest with the executive searcher, for the man you actually want may not be the ideal man as described in the management books.

One other point to remember in connection with hiring outsiders is that the man you select will probably never look as good to you again as he does the day before he reports for work. For some reason (I suppose the psychologists would call it wish fulfillment), we tend to endow these outside candidates with superhuman and almost mystical powers. It is sometimes a letdown when a plain old human being, with the normal virtues and frailties, reports for work.

Another practice which I think requires some reexamination is that of designating an individual as an acting manager. Judging from the frequency that this appellation is used, one would think that half the companies in this country are in the entertainment business!

The usual rationale behind the use of an "acting" title is that the individual has not yet demonstrated his talents for the position, and, until he does, the position is not his to keep. If it is true that he hasn't demonstrated his talents for the position, what then were the criteria used to select him in the first place? Obviously, someone thought that he could do the job, and on that basis I think he should be given it with no strings attached.

The insidious effect of the title acting manager does not extend merely to the victim; it also influences his team. If his men come to perceive that their leader is on trial, they can't help but treat him somewhat differently.

A related instance of poor titling is the use of "assistant to" titles. I have known assistants to the president who were nothing but glorified valets. On the other hand, I have known assistants to the president who were being groomed for the presidency. To me, assistant to is a title utterly devoid of meaning. And since titles are supposed to be one way of identifying the players, I am in favor of eliminating those that are meaningless.

It may seem a little strange to discuss the subject of mergers and acquisitions in a chapter on selection, but

I feel that most mergers and acquisitions hinge on the quality of the management personnel in the company to be acquired. A company may use the acquisition route as a quick means of extending its product line or entering a new industry, but, when it comes to deciding which of several companies to acquire, management talent becomes—or should become—of prime significance. I say "should become" because all too often companies making acquisitions don't really bother to analyze the capabilities of the other company's management team to anywhere near the same degree they analyze the balance sheet. As I mentioned before, I believe it is the quality of management that ultimately makes one company a lot better than another. For this reason, mergers and acquisitions are, in my mind, inextricably lined with the selection process.

It is interesting to note, though, that more than a few acquisitions have been made primarily to get at large sums of cash which have lain idle. To me, assets which are not used as fully as possible are generally a sign of poor management. In that sense, the acquiring company may subsequently find that it has paid a terrifically high price for money alone.

The selection coin has two sides, one being the acquisition of competent personnel, and the other being the necessity, on occasion, to remove an individual who has not fulfilled his promise. Having to take the latter course of action has frequently proved to be the Achilles heel of executives who in other respects are quite competent. It seems to be human nature that most of us want to be liked by those around us, and that seems to apply even to the gruffest of executives. Since removing a man from a job is not very likely to endear us to him, many executives resist the task until the last possible moment, temporizing a little here, rationalizing a little there. Meanwhile, their inaction tends to have a triple-barreled negative effect on the individual and the organization.

First, the individual's performance is hurting the company—otherwise, he wouldn't have been considered for removal—and any delay means further damage. Second, the individual himself is probably not too happy where he is. It has been my experience that most people know when their performance is not up to par. Such knowledge makes them very uncomfortable, probably because it doesn't conform with the image they have (or would like to have) of themselves. I have often seen instances of an executive quitting shortly before he was about to be fired. One interpretation of this phenomenon is that he saw the handwriting on the wall. That may be, but I believe resignations of this type occur not so much to avoid being fired but out of a desire by the individual to remove the psychological dissonance between his poor performance and his self-image.

The third insidious effect of not removing an incompetent executive is the demoralization of subordinate managers. Not only are talented people lower down in the organization blocked from promotion, but the retention of an incompetent executive must cause them some anxiety as to the sort of management the company really has.

I have found that, properly handled, most removals for cause need not be of the traumatic "High Noon" variety, either for the executive being removed or for the person doing the removing. In some cases, the individual can be successfully placed in another, lower job in the company. Let me give you an example.

Many years ago, I was brought into a company from the outside and given the position as vice-president in charge of sales with the promise that I would be made president within a relatively short period of time. One thing the president of the company neglected to tell me when he made the offer, however, was that he had a few years earlier elevated another man to executive vice-president. If he had not actually promised this man the presidency, he certainly left him with the impression that the job would be his.

Shortly after I joined the company, I was given the task of informing the executive vice-president that not only was he not going to be the next president but he was going to have to return to his former job as vice-president and general manager of a division. I didn't want to hurt this man and I certainly didn't want to lose him, because as a division manager he was superlative. In analyzing the situation, I learned that when this man was a division manager, he had been the leading citizen in the small town in which the division was located. He had many friends in this town and in fact wasn't terribly happy about moving to New York when he was made executive vice-president. After establishing close rapport with this individual over a number of months, I called him in and explained to him that I thought it would be better for the company and for him if he were to move back to his old division manager's post. You know, he actually breathed a sigh of relief. He knew that his performance as executive vice-president left much to be desired. He disliked New York and wanted nothing more than to return to the division where his performance had been outstanding and where he had the respect of the entire town. But he was afraid to come in and ask for a transfer because he thought such a request might be construed as a form of weakness. At the same time, he was afraid that he would be discharged from the company and not given a chance to return to his division because of his poor performance as executive vice-president.

Thus, in this situation, an individual was saved and put in a job where he was much more productive. And the whole process was accomplished with very little trauma—either for him or for me.

Of course, not all personnel problems can be solved by moving someone to a different job within the company, and many times an individual has to be removed from the company entirely. In these situations, I have tried whenever possible to avoid an outright discharge and instead have attempted to find another position for the individual at a different company. Let me give you another example.

When the sales vice-presidency in a company of which I was president became vacant, I promoted the most successful division sales manager. I hadn't thought very long or hard about this selection because, after all, the man was a superb division sales manager—the best we had. It was a bad mistake, however. The man turned out to be extremely unhappy as vice-president of sales, and, like most people who are unhappy in their jobs, his performance showed it. On examination, it turned out that this man's first love was selling. He was a true "belly-to-belly" salesman. The only thing that had saved him in his former job as division sales manager was that he could spend a lot of time in the field with his men. But now, as vice-president of sales, he was stuck behind a desk, writing policies, attending committee meetings, developing budgets, and the like —and he detested his new responsibilities.

My first thought was to move him back to his former position as division sales manager, but that position had already been filled and the new incumbent was doing a very good job. Even if the job had been open, it would have been difficult for me to move him into it because it represented a downgrade, and he would have lost his vice-president's title.

I reluctantly decided, therefore, that he would have to be removed from the company. At the same time, I began to consider the type of job in which he would be ideal. That job, I concluded, would have to be the vice-president of sales in a company where such a position was largely a field job. Rather than fire the man, I set out to find a position for him in another company which met those specifications. When I had located the right type of position, I called him in and pointed out why I thought his performance had been unsatisfactory. Then I told him of this vacancy at the other company, which carried a vice-president's title, paid about the same, and involved a good deal of actual selling. He jumped at the opportunity.

In this situation, it became possible to solve a personnel problem without hurting—and actually helping—the individual involved.

In other instances, I have found it useful to employ executive searchers—without the knowledge of the executives involved—as a vehicle for the removal of an executive whose performance was unsatisfactory. If a company has an excellent reputation, it is the constant target of the headhunters. Since one such company I know of was in that position, all I had to do was drop a rumor that Mr. A was unhappy in his work, and within a relatively short period of time the headhunters were besieging him with offers. Such an approach involved no deception since it was invariably true that the individual I wanted to remove really was unhappy—either because he didn't like his job or because he wasn't able to perform it satisfactorily. I never had to give any false references, either, because my competitors never saw fit to ask for them!

In handling managerial personnel, I have always tried to be responsive to the needs of the individual. He has only one life to live, and if making him happy and productive means finding him a job with a competitor, so be it. Such a philosophy, I might add, is not as altruistic as it sounds, for if the individual is not happy he is not likely to be performing well. And if he is not performing well, his departure is a boon to the company as well as to him. Furthermore, this approach helps to create a group of very devoted alumni, and more than once my company became the beneficiary of loyalty repaid through the receipt of additional business from a former employee.

VI

Developing Your People

Suppose you are the sales vice-president of a company located in New York, and you have an opening for a general sales manager in the Chicago office. You have personally selected someone to fill the position, and you are sure he is fully capable of doing the job after some initial training. So far you have not violated any of the management fundamentals.

Shortly before the new general sales manager is to report for work, you call him and say, "Tom, it'll be great to have you on board next month. Why don't you go directly to the Chicago office? When you get there, ask for John Smith. He carries the title of office manager, but he's been around our company for at least a hundred years and he knows absolutely everybody and everything. He'll be expecting you and will get you started off on the right foot. Good luck, and I hope to hear from you soon."

You have now ruined your perfect record and violated a management fundamental. Here's what you should have said: "Tom, it'll be great to have you on board next month. I'm planning to fly out and meet you in the Chicago office the day you report. I'll introduce you to all the sales people and everyone else who will be under your jurisdiction (including John Smith, the office manager), and I'll also set up appointments for us to go out and visit the ten biggest accounts in your territory. That way you can get to know the relationships we have with our customers—how they regard us and how we regard them. I'll be looking forward to seeing you soon."

The management fundamental involved in these examples is that *you must play an important part in the training of each person who is to report to you.* Now, that doesn't mean you have to do all the training yourself. In most cases, the individual will already be skilled in the techniques of his field. Like the Chicago general sales manager, however, you must "bring him up to speed" insofar as the specific position is concerned.

Sometimes, of course—and especially when a manager is switching to a foreign discipline—you must also see that he is trained in the general skills of his new field. I remember the story of the personnel manager who was transferred to the position of sales manager in a coal company. He spent several months reading books and articles on coal, coal mining, and the techniques of selling. To test his new knowledge, he decided to call on a potential customer's purchasing agent. The purchasing agent began asking him some questions. "What," said the P.A. "is the moisture content of your coal?" "Moisture?" queried the salesman. "Why we have pumps running all the time in our mines to keep them perfectly dry. There's no moisture in our coal."

"Well, how about the sulphur content?"

"Not a bit. Our pickers see to that."

"What's the ash content?"

"Every bit of slate, rock, and noncombustible material is removed before the coal is shipped. It has no ash content."

By that time the purchasing agent was really impressed. In fact, he couldn't believe his own ears, so he fired one last question. "What's the BTU content of your coal?"

The new sales manager replied without hesitation, "There's not one damned BTU in a carload!"

Developing good people, as anyone knows who has tried it, requires more patience than skill. Over the short run it is usually easier to do the job yourself, and many of us have fallen into such a trap. Presumably, however, you hired the man to take some of the load off your shoulders, and, that being the case, you have to be willing to invest some time *now* to gain some freedom *later*.

As I mentioned in the chapter on delegation, a manager must be willing to let his subordinates make mistakes, for only in that way will any subordinate truly learn his job. And mistakes—some of them whoppers —will be made.

The proper role a manager should play in developing his subordinate is not to prevent him from making mistakes but to point out his mistakes and thereby give him the feedback he needs to correct his own performance. Recently, teaching machines and programmed instruction have been developed, and these carry the promise of revolutionizing the learning process. The principle which lies behind this teaching method and makes it work is that knowledge of results can improve the rate of learning. Driving a car actually calls for very complex eye-hand coordination and the simultaneous use of several muscle groups. Yet it doesn't take that long to learn to drive a car. The reason is that the would-be driver is automatically given immediate knowledge of the results of his actions. In most cases, he can utilize this knowledge instantly to correct any mistakes he is making.

The learning process is enhanced, therefore, by feedback of performance results. As illustrated in the example of driving a car, however, the feedback should be immediate and not far removed in time.

Unfortunately, many managers have not used this valuable feedback tool to increase the rate at which their subordinates develop. Sometimes, no feedback is given at all, and often what feedback there is consists of a brief, annual performance review. This performance review is usually held in a rather tense atmosphere (somewhat like being called to the principal's office), and the tension is exacerbated when a salary increase is hanging on the results of the review. Small wonder that most people react defensively in their annual performance review sessions.

I have learned in raising my children that praising or punishing a child nine months after a given action (or even three days, for that matter) has absolutely no effect on the child's behavior. Is there any reason to believe that a once-a-year performance review of one's subordinates is going to produce any better results?

I believe in continuous coaching—daily, if necessary. A good coach on a football team doesn't wait until the end of the season to inform his players of their strong and weak points. He does it during and immediately after each game. Nor does a good coach offer criticism in a judgmental and personally humiliating manner. He acts as a mentor and adviser—someone who has the same objectives as his players.

Managers would do well to emulate this type of coach. In my dealings with new subordinates, I have made it a point to hold a performance review every 30 days until I am sure the individual is on the right track. Then I move to reviews every six months. When such reviews are spaced close together, there is not as much riding on any one review and salary actions are not involved in each review session. Thus the atmosphere is less tense and more conducive to learning—which is why the review is being held in the first place. At the same time, I try to hold informal coaching sessions—lasting only five minutes or so—whenever I meet with my subordinates.

What are the criteria that should be used in assessing performance? Until recently, most companies rated an individual on the amount of initiative he displayed, on his creativity, on his appearance, and so on. In effect, these companies measured input and not output. Now there is a growing trend to assess performance primarily on the actual results the man achieved in comparison to what he said he would achieve—that is, his preestablished objectives. I believe this is a healthy development and certainly more comprehensible to the person involved.

In my experience, I have found it helpful to look at the man as a manager and also as a man. Some of the measurements I have used include:

The Man as a Manager
- His knowledge of his industry and his standing in it.
- His performance against his budgets.
- His progress against his competition:
  —Growth in market share.
  —Costs in relation to competitors.
- His plans for the future: Where does he plan to go and how is he going to get there?

■ The strength of his present organization and his plans for improving it.

The Man as a Man
  ■ Leadership characteristics.
  ■ Compatibility.
  ■ Response under stress: Does he crumble under adverse conditions or does he react positively?
  ■ Knowledge of management fundamentals and how to apply them.
  ■ Ingenuity of his approach to problems.

To supplement intracompany development and coaching, I believe that all managers at varying times during their careers should go back to school. Courses can range from 3-day AMA seminars to 12- to 16-week advanced management seminars at such schools as Harvard, M.I.T., and Stanford. These courses serve two basic purposes:

1. To bring the individual up to date on the state of the art in his field.
2. To permit him to discuss his problems with executives in similar positions in other companies.

In my view, the latter purpose is often of primary significance. I have been very active over the years in a group called The Presidents Association, whose membership is comprised entirely of company presidents. At the periodic meetings of this group, formal presentations are made on management development, long-range planning, budgeting, and similar subjects of interest to management. These presentations are very worthwhile, but the main value of having these Presidents Association meetings shows up after the presentation is over, when groups of five or six presidents sit down over a beer and kick the subject matter around. Inevitably, the discussion broadens to include other problems that various chief executives are experiencing. The advice that one receives in these bull sessions is worth its weight in gold. And even if the problem is insoluble, one can take a good deal of comfort in knowing that others are in the same boat.

After attending many Presidents Association meetings, I have developed a means of spotting the presidents who truly delegate responsibilities to subordinates and those who are but one step removed from an ulcer or a coronary. Those who delegate never call their offices during the entire week of the meeting, and they receive no calls from their offices. The others jump up at every coffee break and meal period and phone their office to "see what's new" and whether "John is doing what I told him to do." They then return to the meeting with an air that implies, "If I weren't around, the company would fall apart." They're probably right, but for the wrong reasons!

Another development tool which I have found to be extremely useful is the management institute. Selected middle-level managers with demonstrated high potential are periodically invited to the company's headquarters and there given presentations by the president of the company and each of his vice-presidents. The subject matter includes the state of the business, the outlook for the future, and status reports on each major function. A management institute of this type has a number of values:

- It gives status recognition to those invited to attend and makes them feel part of top management.
- It allows the attendees to get to know the company's top brass.
- It gives the attendees the information they need to know in order to run their own units.
- It is a source of valuable suggestions for the company's top managers—who, after all, don't have an exclusive patent on management knowledge.
- It provides the occasion when, in after-hours sessions, the attendees exchange ideas, discuss problems, and generally help create a degree of synergism in the company.

An idea currently in vogue is to have at least five or six qualified candidates ready to take each key management job. The implication is that any company that doesn't have such in-depth management is not very well run. I believe this approach, although deceptively appealing, is without merit.

I remember that the first time I wanted to appoint

someone as president of the company of which I was chairman, there was only one man ready. I gave him the job, but I didn't train him properly. (As I mentioned earlier, I learned management fundamentals the hard way!) Eighteen months later he was dead, and I can't help feeling that his unhappiness in the job was a primary cause of his death.

I had no choice but to resume the presidency. However, as a result of that experience, I began to groom a number of men for the job. Within three years I had six men who were so equally ready to take on the president's job that I had to ask a committee of the board of directors to help me make the selection. Now, you might think this was an enviable situation in which to be. But it wasn't. I realized I would end up with one happy man and five very dissatisfied ones. It wasn't long afterward that almost all of the five "losers" left the company.

The point here is that you cannot groom a man for a job without creating the expectation in him that he will receive it. Even though he may have been perfectly happy in his job before you started to prepare him for a higher one, he is unlikely to remain happy if he doesn't get that higher job.

My view is that a company should have one fully qualified candidate for each key management position. Alternate candidates who still need further development should be identified, but their development should continue at a normal pace. Under such an approach, it is of course possible that the single designated candidate will quit and leave a void in the replacement plan, but in that event the secondary candidate or candidates can be put on an enriched development diet. I think this is a better approach, on balance, than "storing nuts for the winter" and demoralizing some perfectly happy executives.

VII

Controlling the Organization

*I*n an earlier chapter, we discussed the need for managers to delegate decisions down to the lowest level in the organization where they can be made intelligently. But delegation cannot work by itself. The more you delegate to your subordinates, the more you will have to control your organization to insure that every decision you have delegated is made by the man who is supposed to make it at the time it is supposed to be made.

Delegation without control is abdication. Unfortunately, "control" is a negatively charged word—especially in a democratic society. "Control" smacks of "big brother is watching you," and it implies that one has less freedom to act than would be the case were there no controls. Of course, most people don't mind doing the controlling. What they resent is being controlled.

Let me give you an example of how *not* to control an organization. Mr. A was playing golf on Sunday afternoon with one of his competitors. As he stepped to the tee and started his swing, his competitor casually remarked, "I hear your sales aren't going so well." Now, the only reason Mr. A's competitor made that remark was to foul up his golf game—and he succeeded admirably. But Mr. A couldn't stop thinking about the remark, and all night long he tossed and turned. The minute he hit the office Monday morning, he sent for his sales manager. "What's the matter with our sales?" he demands to know. "Nothing's the matter. We've got orders coming out of our ears," the sales manager replies, but, feeling that he should say something negative to answer an implied negative question, he adds, "Of course, I'm having a little trouble getting deliveries out of the manufacturing department on some of our new products." Mr. A says, "Oh! So that's the trouble." He immediately summons his manufacturing manager. "What's the matter with your department? The sales manager says he's got plenty of orders but you aren't turning the new products out fast enough." The manufacturing manager replies, "Boss, I'd love to make the new products but I can't get the specifications out of the engineering department."

So in comes the engineering manager. Mr. A says, "Why haven't you given the manufacturing manager the specifications he needs for those new products?"

The engineering manager replies, "I'd love to give him his specifications. But I need two more engineers, and the controller won't let me hire them."

"Now we're at the heart of the matter," Mr. A thinks to himself. Naturally, the controller is summoned immediately. "All right, why have you refused to give the engineering manager the two specifications engineers he needs?"

The controller, looking both puzzled and hurt, answers, "If I gave the engineering manager two more engineers, he'd be over budget, and *you* are the one who set the budget!"

Controls are not things to be used during a crisis; they are designed to prevent a crisis from occurring.

What are the controls in your organization? First and most important, controls are your subordinate managers. Properly selected, properly trained, properly organized, and properly informed, they constitute your first line of control because they make the decisions they are supposed to make at the time they are supposed to make them.

Your second set of controls consists of various policies concerning aspects of the business, such as hiring policies, budget policies, approval of budget variances, marketing policies, and capital expenditure policies. In a way, these policies are simply an extension of the position descriptions for broad groups of executives. Together, policies and position descriptions combine to place a fence around the executive's decision-making area.

Some people confuse controls with what I like to call *statistical indicators*. Take the 707 aircraft, for example. The pilot sits at the controls, which he uses to maneuver the plane, increase the speed of the turbines, and so on. Staring him in the face are literally hundreds of instruments. One of them is a fuel gauge, which tells him the amount of fuel in his tanks. If that gauge reads "empty," there isn't a thing the pilot can do about it, and the plane is bound to come down to earth. The fuel gauge is not a control in any sense of the word; it is a statistical indicator which gives the pilot certain information about the airplane.

Industry also utilizes numerous statistical indicators —charts, graphs, budget status reports, sales reports by product line, and manufacturing costs analyses and the like. These are highly important because they advise the manager as to whether his controls are working and how well they are working, but these charts, graphs, and reports cannot in themselves control anything or anybody.

As I mentioned earlier, your principal controls are your subordinate managers. Armed with statistical indicators and the power to make decisions, they can see to it that their organization is under proper control. They can, but sometimes they don't. My experience has been that man's capacity to rationalize is infinite. And, like some pilots who refuse to believe there really is no fuel left in their tanks, many managers refuse to believe what their statistical indicators are telling them. As a result, some of these indicators must also be furnished to a manager's boss and to certain staff functions.

To illustrate the subjectivity with which statistical indicators are sometimes interpreted, let me give you two examples.

One of my manufacturing managers decided as one of his objectives for the year to make a certain component for $1.86 each. At first he was right on target. But a few months later I received a standard unit cost report prepared by the controller's department showing that the cost of this component had risen to $1.92. So I called my manufacturing manager, who was located in Chicago, and asked him what the story was. He replied indignantly, "Boss, don't you read the newspapers? We had a terrific blizzard in Chicago last week and 40 percent of the workforce couldn't get to the plant until one o'clock in the afternoon. That's what caused the unit cost to increase." So I thanked him and apologized for bothering him. Several weeks passed, and the latest edition of the unit cost report showed that the cost of this component had increased once more to $1.96. So I called my manufacturing manager once again. "I've read every newspaper," I said, "and there wasn't any blizzard in Chicago last week!" I went on to ask him for analyses of his raw material, labor, and overhead costs and a report on when he was going to get his unit costs back in line.

In another case, a sales vice-president decided not to inform me that his West Coast orders had decreased $50,000 per week. Now, he wasn't trying to deceive me. He knew, from meeting with his West Coast sales manager, that the purchasing agent of a big aerospace company, which ordered $50,000 of products each week, was out sick with the Hong Kong flu—or some such ailment. He also knew that this purchasing agent insisted on signing every purchase order himself. Therefore, he saw no reason to worry me when it was obvious that all the back purchase orders would be released as soon as the purchasing agent returned to work.

My controller, however, did inform me that orders were showing a significant decrease on the West Coast, and so I called in my vice-president of sales and asked him for an explanation. Still not telling me the real reason, he gave me the speech that all harassed sales managers commit to memory against the day their supervisor turns on the heat. "Boss," he said, "why do you look at the figures every week? Don't you know that in this business we have peaks and valleys? Some weeks we get the orders, and some weeks we don't. If you would just tell the controller to give you a report once a month, you'd save yourself a lot of heartache."

Well, I let a few weeks go by, but the order reports still continued to show a $50,000-per-week decline. So I called my vice-president of sales in once again and said, "Look, somebody is beating me to death, and if it isn't you it must be the referee!" I told him to submit a report to me within three days, detailing the weaknesses in incoming orders on the West Coast and informing me of what he planned to do to rectify the situation.

In preparing this report, the sales vice-president called the West Coast aerospace company directly and asked after the health of the purchasing agent. He found, to his dismay, that the purchasing agent was not sick at all. He had been fired eight weeks ago and replaced by a man who didn't think too much of our company's products!

These examples vividly illustrate the need for statistical control reports to be given not only to the manager doing the controlling but also to his boss and key staff personnel.

A word of caution, however. While the manager who is doing the controlling needs highly detailed statistical indicators, his supervisor can and should get along with considerably less detail. The submission of overly detailed reports to levels higher than the one performing the control function is an invitation to interference by the people at these higher levels. Thus the president of a company can profitably utilize a sales report which shows sales by major product groupings and major geographical areas. But this report should not show sales for each and every product the company

makes and for each and every sales district and salesman. These detailed statistical indicators should be
submitted only to those managers in the sales department who are responsible for controlling individual
product sales and sales in each district office.

Another caution to be observed with statistical indicators is to be sure that the manager doing the controlling is the first to receive the indicators for his area. Because these indicators are often prepared by an independent function such as the controller's department, it
often occurs that even junior staff personnel receive statistical reports before the manager does. This in turn
sometimes leads to an attack on the controlling manager before he has even received his reports and had a
chance to formulate actions needed to correct any deficiencies revealed in the reports.

Statistical indicators, like coaching one's subordinates, are excellent means of conveying knowledge of
results to managers who are responsible for controlling
those results.

In addition, statistical indicators help to improve
the decision-making process in still another way when
the person making the decisions improves his performance because he knows that the results of those decisions are being monitored by others. Every commercial
jet aircraft in the United States carries a flight recorder
which details every maneuver the pilot makes. This recorder, which cannot be reached by the flight crew,
can be used to determine whether a pilot acted precip-

itately during a flight or in any other way endangered the safety of the passengers or the aircraft. I cannot help but feel that commercial pilots fly just a little better because of the presence of that flight recorder.

It should be obvious from our discussion that, with proper controls, delegation need not be an anxiety-provoking experience to the individual doing the delegating. In a way, he can have his cake and eat it too. He can take some of the load off his back and get better and faster decisions made by people who are more knowledgeable than he and closer to where the action is.

To the would-be but fearful delegator, let me offer an example. You have decided that you really ought to delegate considerable decision-making authority and autonomy to the Los Angeles sales manager. But you are having trouble sleeping at night because you think, "What if the guy fouls up? I'm 3,000 miles away and can't move fast enough to correct the problem." Well, you needn't worry if you have instituted a good set of controls. The first of these is the Los Angeles manager himself, a man whom you have personally selected and in whose training you have played an important part. He has a position description which tells him what decisions he can make and what decisions he can't make. In short, he knows his job and is ready to do it.

You then set out to build some additional fences around the Los Angeles manager's decision-making powers. You issue a policy statement that permits only salaried salesmen to be utilized. Now, the Los Angeles manager would dearly love to violate that policy because he can't afford to send a salaried salesman over to the intermountain area, and the use of a manufacturer's representative would gross him $100,000 worth of sales with only a nominal 5 percent commission charge. But he won't violate that policy, if for no other reason than because it is in writing and a violation would be impossible to justify.

Then you give him a budget. This control prevents him from overspending without your knowing it. Although you may indulge in fantasies that your Los Angeles manager is out burning up the expense account with Hollywood starlets every night, have no fear; his budget won't permit it, and he won't exceed his budget without your permission if he wants to remain with the company.

The Los Angeles manager is also fenced in by company ethical policies and by legal policies, such as the Robinson-Patman act, which states that he can't sell to one customer at a price which differs from that offered to another customer unless he can justify the difference in terms of cost.

So, how is the Los Angeles manager going to give the company away? He can't because you have given him all the decision-making tools he needs and have established controls to see that he uses these tools properly.

As indicated earlier, the budget is one of management's primary control tools. It should not be established lightly, neither should deviations from it be taken lightly.

I believe that the budget should be drawn in a meeting with one's entire team. All the facts necessary to arrive at an intelligent budget should be brought forth at this meeting. Questions that should be answered include these:

- What is expected to happen in the general economy? In regional and local economies?
- What new products are expected to be introduced by our competitors?
- What new products are we going to introduce?
- What level of sales can we reasonably expect to achieve—and why?
- What changes can we expect in our direct manufacturing costs and overhead? Typical items to be considered are the impact of union settlements, increases for salaried personnel, manpower staffing levels, raw materials prices, and so on.

On the basis of the facts and projections that emerge from this team meeting, the budget can be intelligently established. And, since each team member was given an opportunity to contribute to the end product, there is a much greater chance that the budget will be accepted as a realistic and meaningful document to be followed rather than subverted.

As the year progresses, the actual results obtained should be periodically reviewed against the budget. Personally, I favor a review every three months coupled with a projection of what is likely to happen over the ensuing twelve months. In that manner the company is always looking ahead for twelve months (and, of course, five and ten years ahead also with the intermediate-term plans that have been drawn).

In administering his budget, a manager must be prepared to face pressure from his subordinates to decrease the original budget in the event that actual results have fallen significantly below budgeted results. Some companies will do this, and they justify such an approach in the interests of greater accuracy and realism. Personally, I will never allow a sales or profit budget to be decreased because I believe that such an approach takes the pressure off one's subordinates to perform up to original expectations. Let me give an example. The budget established at the beginning of the year calls for the sale of a million hockey pucks. Actual sales fall significantly below the budget, and by May it becomes obvious that the very best the company will do that year is to sell 800,000 hockey pucks. Naturally, the sales vice-president thinks the budget should be redrawn to call for 800,000 units. In that manner, if he actually sells 800,000 he can say with a straight face, "I made my budget." If you as the manager accede to this request, you will remove a major incentive for the sales vice-president to "do the impossible" and sell the originally projected number of hockey pucks. More-over, since next year's budget is in large part predicated on this year's sales, you will have enabled him to come to you, again with a straight face, and say, "Boss, next year I'm budgeting sales of a million hockey pucks—that's a 25 percent increase over this year, you know!" So, by changing the budget, not only will you have lost a potential opportunity this year, but you have allowed an inordinately low target to be established for next year.

I don't mind adding a third column to the budget to take care of problems of this type, however. In addi-tion to the original budget figure and the actual results to date, a third column, current estimate for the year, can be added. This approach may mollify some of the anxious team members, but it doesn't take them com-pletely off the hook.

If any further proof is required of the justice of re-fusing to decrease a budget once it is drawn, try and name the last time, if ever, that your team asked to *in-crease* the original budget figure because sales to date were running 50 percent ahead of budget.

Two areas of the business that require careful con-trol are research and engineering. At one time or an-other, most presidents start to wonder whether all those thousands of research dollars are beginning to pay off in salable products. So they call in Dr. Von Schlumpf, their eminent research director, whom they paid dearly to obtain from the halls of ivy, and ask him how things are going. The good doctor, of course, has been thoroughly schooled (like his sales manager counterpart) in putting down the boss. So he clears his throat, adjusts his glasses so he is looking down at the president, and in his most polished foreign accent says, "Well, things are going quite well, and we have uncovered some promising new avenues of investigation. Of course, I can't go into the technical details because your background just wouldn't permit it."

Many company presidents who used to be proud that they graduated from the Harvard Business School feel very uneasy and terribly ignorant in the face of this superior intellect and sheepishly end the meeting without going any further.

This is a mistake. It may take a doctorate in physics to perform research, but it takes only an inquiring mind to understand the implications of that research. I have known presidents of large aerospace firms who never took one technical course in school and who, before assuming the presidency, thought that a vertical stabilizer was some sort of undergarment worn by women. Yet they refused to be cowed by their technical managers. If they got lost in a deliberately obscure explanation, they weren't afraid to say, "Now take me through that once again and slowly."

I believe that research is as amenable to planning and control as any other part of the business. I have found it useful to prepare a research budget for each and every project to be undertaken or continued each year. In addition to the submission of a research budget for that project, I ask my research director to indicate the purpose of the project in terms of possible end results, the probability of accomplishment, and the technical milestones that should be met during the year. Then a review of progress against this budget is made every three months. If a project is not meeting its milestones and the money could be used more profitably in some more promising research area, I do not hesitate to cancel the project then and there. Without such an approach, it is too easy to be bled to death.

An additional and excellent statistical indicator is what I have termed an *operations review meeting*. At regular intervals, a manager's entire team is assembled. One member is selected in advance to discuss his area of the business, and he is made the chairman of that meeting. The team member's presentation is built around four major points:

1. Here's where we are: a discussion of the results actually attained to date.
2. Here's where we said we would be: a discussion of preestablished objectives.
3. Here are the reasons for the variance.
4. Here's what we are going to do about it.

There are two basic reasons for having the whole team, rather than the manager alone, hear this departmental review. First, the other team members can learn how their performance is affecting the department undergoing review. Second, if any unjust accusations are being made as to deficiencies on the part of other team members, these can be corrected on the spot. In this way, an operations review meeting can be a synergistic experience for the whole team.

Some managers shy away from such operations review meetings because they fear that these meetings will degenerate into backbiting sessions, with the team trying to impress the boss by taking potshots at the member delivering the presentation. My experience is that this happens only infrequently and is quickly corrected. People may like to take potshots at others, but they rarely like to be on the receiving end. And that is just where they will find themselves when it is their turn to lead a meeting, if they start attacking their peers unnecessarily.

Let your team do the talking. Other managers shy away from such operations review meetings because they feel that the members will gradually turn the session into a forum for the boss to air his own opinions. This can easily happen and should be avoided. The purpose of the operations review meeting is to hear your team members' views, not to wow them with your brilliance. You will undoubtedly experience pressure from your subordinates to say what you think, because they know you like to hear yourself talk. And, if they can find out which way you are heading, they will never be in an exposed position. You must therefore politely decline to offer your views—at least until everyone around the table has had a chance to comment.

You must also avoid giving serious criticism during the meeting to the team member delivering the presentation. Nothing is more humiliating than to be chewed out in the presence of one's peers. Should major criticism be necessary, take the man aside after the meeting and talk to him privately.

One of the mechanical problems I used to experience with operations review meetings was in determining an acceptable time to meet. My team members didn't want to meet Tuesday through Friday because they wanted to be on the road. Nor did they want to meet Monday morning because they wanted to read the mail that came in over the weekend. So, by a process of elimination, I settled on a Monday afternoon meeting time, and it worked out quite well.

Another technique I found quite successful in handling operations review meetings is to require that the team member delivering the presentation write it beforehand and circulate copies to the other team members and me prior to the meeting. I have found few things as irritating as sitting in a meeting while the speaker drones through a 40-page report. By the time he is finished, I have forgotten half of what he said. If on the other hand the team members can read the report before the meeting, a lengthy declamation can be avoided and the team can immediately get down to the essentials of the report.

There is also another advantage to insisting that reports be written. The act of writing a report guarantees that it will be a better product. The thoughts and ideas the individual develops stare back at him from the printed page, and logical errors as well as omissions are more readily revealed.

❋ ❋ ❋ ❋

To summarize, a company is properly controlled when its managers are properly selected and trained; when they know what they are supposed to do and when they are supposed to do it; when proper policy controls have been inaugurated; and when valid statistical indicators have been established to measure progress and spot potential problem areas while there is still time to make corrections.

VIII

Communication

Some time ago, a psychologist was brought into a company which was experiencing a number of organizational and personnel problems. His task was to interview the company's managers and determine what was wrong. He started with the lowest-level foreman, and in his very first interview he asked, "What do you think of the treatment you are receiving from top management?" The foreman snorted, "Treatment? They treat us like we were a mushroom farm." "What do you mean by that?" asked the psychologist. The foreman replied, "Well, they keep us in the dark, they feed us horse manure, and they can us!"

Failure to establish proper communication among the management team members is a problem which seems to be endemic. I am not a psychologist by background, but I suspect that there is a good deal of status —or one-upmanship—attached to knowing something someone else doesn't know.

When I initially became president of one company, it was very small and I was a neophyte. The first time I received a quarterly earnings report, I traveled to each of our three plants and asked the plant manager to assemble the employees in the cafeteria. I then spoke for about ten minutes and discussed the report. I also gave the employees some very general information on the outlook for the near future.

When I arrived in the home office and attended a meeting of the board of directors a few days later, I was thoroughly chewed out for discussing the quarterly earnings report with the employees. One director said scathingly, "Why did you go and do such a fool thing? Now the employees will all want more money." I replied to the board's criticism, "First of all, the employees all want more money now. They will always want more money, whether the company is making a profit or a loss. Second, I have found that a very large percentage of our employees are literate—they can actually read and write. Everything I told them is going to be in the local newspapers tomorrow morning. By giving them the information a few days early, I helped them to feel they were on the inside."

For this reason, I am very much in favor of having company presidents and other top managers meet periodically with all or at least a part of the employees in their organization. In small companies, all the employees, including production and clerical workers, should be invited to these meetings. In larger companies, it may be feasible to include only the supervisor-foreman groups. In these meetings the president should discuss the state of the company, giving the employees as much information—both good and bad—as he is legally and strategically able to do. Meetings of this type serve several purposes.

- They *inform*—and that, after all, is the name of the game in communication.
- They help to get across the company point of view. The company's competitors, its unions, and other special-interest groups are all actively telling their story. Faced with such an environment, therefore, it is hardly timely for a company president to start following the old "modesty is a virtue" adage.
- They demonstrate the president's interest in and concern for his *total* company team. The Urban Coalition, a group which is dedicated to removing some of the inequalities of American life, uses the slogan, "Give a damn." It is appropriate here also.

There is just no point in withholding information from people when they are going to find out anyway or when they have a need to know. If you don't tell them someone else will, and, more often than not, the information they get will be misinformation.

Nature abhors a vacuum, and an information vacuum is no exception. It is going to be filled one way or

A Third of Shoppers Purchase Take-Out Foods

CAMDEN, N.J.—A new study sponsored jointly by the Food Marketing Institute (FMI) and the Campbell Soup Co. says that sales of take-out food from supermarkets has reached $14.4 billion annually, and is expected to continue to expand at a rapid pace.

Eight out of 10 American households report buying take-out food at least once in a four-week period, with the average household purchasing a total of $16.50 per week, reports the study. Total take-out food purchases from all outlets has reached $62.4 billion annually, meaning that supermarkets have almost 25 percent of that annual business.

The survey, conducted for FMI and Campbell Soup by Lieberman Research Inc., indicated that of those questioned, 30 percent reported having purchased take out food at a supermarket. Seventy-six percent of those asked said they purchased take-out food from a fast food restaurant, while 66 percent did so at a pizza parlor, 33 percent at an ethnic restaurant, and 29 percent at a delicatessen. (These figures add up to more than 100 percent because people bought take-out food more than once, and not always at the same type of outlet.)

According to Monica Wood, Campbell's manager of marketing research, the fact that "supermarkets offer a greater variety of healthful foods" allows that industry to successfully compete for fast-food dollars. "We think they could easily pull ahead of the fast-food chains in years to come."

Other findings include these:

☐ 78 percent of decisions to purchase take-out food are classified as impulse decisions;

☐ 82 percent of take-out meals are eaten at home, with the remaining 18 percent consumed at work;

☐ Hamburgers remain the the most popular take-out food, followed by pizza, prepared chicken, sandwiches, baked or fried fish, and prepared salads; and

☐ Chinese and Mexican food are the most popular ethnic take-out foods, with roughly five out of 10 people questioned saying that they would choose ethnic take out.

The study also suggests that retailers looking to appeal to the prime consumers of take-out food should do so by catering to their upscale images of themselves. Heavy buyers of take-out food see themselves as modern, successful, career-oriented, pressured and sophisticated, while light buyers of take-out food view themselves as home-centered, cost conscious, old-fashioned, and traditional.

t must have had

the **1987 Country Music Association Awards.**
r live prime-time TV Special on CBS — filled with
e idea commercials.

RAFT Hometown, USA, Promotion:
ft recipe ideas to drive people down every aisle of
re.

3 recipes in 17,000,000 issues of
ide magazine that night.

3 recipes in **Hometown, USA, store folders** for
splays.

another. Take the case of Joe, one of the foremen at a manufacturing plant. Not four feet from his office is a bulletin board, and anything of importance is placed on this board by the personnel department. That is the workers' only source of communication, and it is Joe's only source of communication as well. He is a member of management—at least theoretically—but no one seems willing to take the time to keep him informed.

One day a worker comes to Joe's office and asks, "What about this rumor I heard?" Joe replies, "I don't know what you're talking about." An hour later another worker approaches Joe. "What about this rumor I heard?" Again, "I don't know what you're talking about." The process is repeated several times, and finally Joe becomes exasperated and replies to his ninth questioner, "I'll be damned if I know. Nobody tells me anything around this company." He certainly can't be considered a good representative of management at this point.

Having received no answer to their questions, Joe's workers do the next best thing: They go to the union steward and ask him. Now, the union steward doesn't know the answer either, but he is not about to admit it because that would be bad for business. So he gives them an answer—any answer—and very likely the wrong answer. The information vacuum has been filled!

Unless there is some compelling legal or strategic reason not to divulge certain information, it should be divulged—and freely. People want information, and the quality doesn't seem to be nearly as important as the quantity. From a management standpoint, however, quality of information is often all-important, and in such cases the managers had better fill the void themselves, or someone else will fill it for them.

The same applies to dealing with one's own management team. In this area of communication especially, there is no reason not to be utterly frank. Of course, a few items must always be kept secret for a while, because of legal or strategic reasons, but my experience has been that they are truly few in number. Everything else can and should be divulged to the management team. After all, how can you expect your team to operate at peak efficiency if you insist on playing with a stacked deck? Yet I have met too many managers who, like children, play the game, "I've got a secret, and I'm not going to tell you!"

Another point to remember is that your management team is ultimately no different from a group of the lowest-classified production workers in its desire for information. If you leave an information vacuum, it will be filled just as readily—and with just as much misinformation—at the highest as at the lowest organization levels.

There are many types of communications, including the employee house organ, memoranda, and policy statements, but I personally think that there is nothing better than face-to-face communication. That is why I am so fond of operations review meetings.

With face-to-face communication, there is opportunity for a sort of nonverbal feedback to the communicator. He can develop an awareness of how his thoughts are being received, and such an awareness has saved more than one manager from making a drastic mistake in his choice of words and phraseology. In addition, the listeners can raise questions and inject their points of view. Further, the listener can also use nonverbal cues thrown off by the speaker to form a better impression of the value and importance of the material being communicated as well as the sincerity of the speaker. I realize that some company presidents would rather be heard but not seen, but I think that over the long run such isolation is a mistake.

Now, this doesn't mean that a company president should go overboard in his desire to be communicative. Some presidents I know have almost literally turned themselves into walking public relations firms. Hardly a week goes by without having the president's picture appear in a major magazine. Speeches to virtually any group that will listen are commonplace. Ostensibly, such a whirlwind of communication is designed to enhance the company's image. If in the process the company's image gets weaker and weaker and the president's personal image gets stronger and stronger, well, one can't foresee every eventuality!

It is perfectly acceptable—even desirable—for the president to indulge in a certain amount of image-building for the company. But it is important to remember that the president's main job is to be a manager, and, once his public relations activities start to cut into the time he should be spending on managing, they should be curtailed.

For the same reason, I am skeptical of the open-door policy or the posture that some presidents adopt of answering their own telephones. On paper, these gestures to industrial democracy and good communication make a good deal of sense. But, if they are followed to the letter, the inevitable result is an erosion of the time that the president should be using for more important managerial activities. The fact is, I've yet to see an open door that was really open for very long, simply because the president discovers that he can't afford the time. Unfortunately, to make a promise and then not deliver is far worse from a morale standpoint than not to have made the promise in the first place.

What, then, is the president's proper communications role? First, he must communicate with his management team and with all the other employees in the company. Face-to-face meetings, as mentioned earlier, are extremely valuable in this regard. In addition, the president can use the employee house organ to get his message across. This newspaper or magazine provides the president with an excellent forum and an entree not only to the employees but also to relatives, customers, and suppliers. The president, however, should use the house organ *only when he really has something to say*. This means that he shouldn't permit himself to be signed up for a weekly column, because to do so will probably result in "turning off" his readership.

While on the subject of employee house organs, let me add my belief that they are not a waste of money, but can be a valuable morale-building device, especially when they contain numerous pictures and names of employees. After all, company presidents don't have a corner on the market for vanity! For that reason, I favor inexpensive but frequent throwaway newspapers, rather than expensive but infrequent glossy magazines. In that way more pictures and names can be used for the same cost.

Another and more informal area of internal communication is socializing with groups of company personnel. This area has some possibilities but far more pitfalls in my opinion. I have no objection to a president's attending the employee picnic and even saying a few words, but he should do so only by invitation of the employees. It is their picnic (the company can subsidize it but it should be organized and run by the employees), and if the president intrudes without invitation no good can come of it. In such a case, it would be far better for him to stay home.

Executive socializing is another dangerous pastime, especially insofar as the president or any team leader is concerned. The problem lies not with the executives, who simply extend their business discussions into the evening, but with their wives. My experience has been that these lovely ladies, when brought together in groups, develop the art of intrigue and political manipulation to a degree that would put Rasputin to shame! More than one company president I know has decided to promote an able executive only to be confronted by a withering barrage of criticism from his wife, who, in conjunction with the other executives' wives, has already decided that another man—for reasons that are usually obscure—is far better for the job. It is for these reasons that I moved to New Jersey when most of my management team moved to Connecticut!

The president also has a vital role to play in communications outside the company, although, as I said before, some temperance is required. First, the president often can be of indirect assistance in obtaining new business for the company. I say "indirect" because he presumably has a sales vice-president to whom he has delegated the actual responsibility for obtaining new business. Nevertheless, the president is often in a position to meet socially with his counterparts in customer firms. During these encounters he can talk generally about the company's plans and its new products, and he can listen with a sympathetic ear to the customer's problems. He should do no more than that, however. When it comes to specific contract terms, delivery commitments, or the like, it is time to turn the matter over to the sales vice-president, who has the responsibility—and, more importantly—the expertise.

The president plays another communications role in his dealings with the public. He is the prime spokesman for the company, and as such he is likely to be barraged with requests. The news media want interviews. The investment community wants information. Industry associations ask for speeches, and so do public-spirited groups in locations where the company has facilities. To a degree, he should try to be responsive to this hunger for information. But, again, he must consider that his main job is managing.

The president also meets the public at annual meetings. Here again, he has an opportunity to present the company's point of view—and he should take it. Regrettably, however, I have seen too many presidents who view annual meetings not as an opportunity to communicate but as a minefield seeded with dissident stockholders. These presidents spend their time thinking up defensive answers to questions that may never even be asked. My experience with annual meetings has taught me to distinguish between dissident stockholders who have a legitimate grievance—or at least a legitimate question—and those publicity seekers who use annual meetings as self-serving forums. The people in the first group deserve sincere treatment, and with rather little effort they can be given such treatment. The people in the second group cannot—and will not—be ignored, but I have found that the other stockholders at the meeting will usually handle the problem themselves if the publicity seekers become too obstreperous.

❧   ❧   ❧   ❧

To summarize, proper and timely communications are vitally important for every company. Unless there is a compelling legal or strategic reason not to communicate information, it should always be communicated. One way or another, the information vacuum is going to be filled, so why not fill it the right way?

IX

Compensation

You have personally selected your management team members. You have played an important role in their training. You have given them position descriptions which spell out the decisions they can make. You demand high standards of performance and remove anyone who doesn't meet them.

Why, pray tell, does a person work for you 50 to 60 hours per week and be held accountable for his decisions? Certainly, he gets a lot of kicks out of what he is doing. But he could also get a lot of kicks out of other positions, where accountability for decisions was less traceable to a single individual. Challenge itself is of course important, but I believe that a fundamental reason why people enter business is to make money.

Enter the psychologists from stage left. They speak: "Our research shows that money doesn't motivate anybody; executives will not work harder to earn more money." I remember seeing the show *Gypsy;* in that play there was a song featuring one striptease artist telling another that, with properly rigged electric lights, she could really draw the crowds. The title of the song was, "You Gotta Have a Gimmick." Well, as far as I am concerned, the psychologists have come up with a marvelous gimmick when they say that money no longer motivates. In fact, their gimmick is so successful that they are in great demand by conclaves of executives who go in for self-flagellation. The schedules of these psychologists are so crowded with speaking engagements that, when you call one to ask him to speak, his first question is, "How much?"

I can, however, verify part of what the psychologists are saying. I have talked in my time with many company presidents, and I must confess that I have yet to find one who will admit he would work any harder if the company paid him more money. On the other hand, suppose the president's board of directors took this statement at face value and allowed his salary to fall below what other companies were paying. Now, executive searchers are assiduous readers of proxy statements, and it wouldn't take them long to conclude that this president was underpaid. Shortly thereafter, he would become the target of other companies looking for presidents. And, although it is true that he wouldn't work any harder for more money, he might be very interested in working just as hard but receiving a 50 percent increase in compensation provided by another company.

In my view, people do not work for money per se. They work for the things money can buy. Let's take three executives in a company. One is young and unmarried. He loves fast, shiny automobiles, and his goal in life is to purchase a red, 350-horsepower racing machine. A salary increase of $5,000 to this man is not 5,000 one-dollar bills; it's a new racing car.

Take another executive. He has been married only a few months, and he is still starry-eyed. To him, the greatest thing in life is a little Cape Cod home with a white picket fence around it and roses growing along the fence. A $5,000 raise to this man represents part of the payments on that little Cape Cod home, not 5,000 one-dollar bills.

Take the senior executive who is within three years of retirement. His dream is to have a little cottage in Florida right on the Atlantic Ocean, where he can fish and sail to his heart's content. Again, a $5,000 raise means not 5,000 one-dollar bills but that little Florida cottage.

As far as I am concerned, money is still a motivator. Of course, it is not the only motivator, but to my way of thinking, it is the *prime* motivator.

Since most of my career has been in marketing, I have retained considerable interest in the field of salesmen's compensation. To me, what passes for sales compensation in many companies is an utter travesty.

Early in my career, I was employed by a publishing company as an advertising space salesman. One day, the sales vice-president came to me and said, "Mitchell, we have devised a sales compensation plan which will really spur your effort. I am going to give you 10 percent of the first $50,000 of advertising that you sell; 7.5 percent of the second $50,000 of bookings; and 5 percent of the third $50,000 and everything above that." He then paused to receive the tribute of a grateful subordinate.

Unfortunately, I didn't oblige him. "I have a counterproposal," I said. "Give me 5 percent of the first $50,000 of bookings that I bring into the agency; 7.5 percent of the second $50,000 of bookings; and 10 percent of the third $50,000 and everything above that." The vice-president sputtered, "But you'll never be able to live on the first $50,000 of bookings." I said, "I don't intend to. I intend to live on the 10 percent above the third $50,000 of bookings!"

Now, almost everyone in management knows that the cost curve is rather flat and the profit curve is rather steep. Essentially, a business doesn't make any money until a sufficient volume of production has been achieved. Thereafter, the company begins to make money at a very rapidly increasing rate. While you are digesting this, consider also just why it is that a company designs a sales incentive compensation plan in the first place. For openers, let's take the two key words of the title of most companies' plans: "sales" and "incentive." The company is obviously giving the individual an incentive to increase his sales. Now, why would the company want to do that? Presumably, because greater sales lead to the attainment of certain objectives that are of interest to the company. About the only objective that I can think of in this connection is profit!

Now, if the company wants to spur sales in order to get on that steeply accelerating portion of the profit curve, why is it that the company offers the salesman a smaller and smaller percentage of the increased sales that he achieves?

I think I know part of the answer. Years ago, I was vice-president of sales in a soft drink company. Now, another company had an inordinately high share of the soft drink market. Our goal was to make some inroads in this market share, and to do this we developed a rather simple incentive plan for our district managers. We paid them two cents per case override on each case of soft drinks they sold.

During the first few years after we introduced this plan, none of the district managers made very much money. But, eventually, as a result of what I like to think of as an innovative marketing strategy, sales began to improve markedly. And so did the compensation of the district managers. At that point, the president of the company showed up in my office. "We've got to change the compensation arrangements of those district managers," he said. "They're making too much money." I said, "Wait a minute. Three years ago we couldn't afford to pay them one cent per case override, much less the two cents we are paying currently. Now we're making a pile of profit. So how is it that we can no longer afford to pay two cents per case override?" Well, that answer didn't really mollify the president, but he evidently couldn't think of any devastating comeback, so he retired to his office. I didn't hear from him for several months.

Then one day he showed up in my office again, waving the latest sales compensation report under my nose. "We have absolutely got to change the arrangements of those district managers," he said. "Their compensation is completely out of line." I replied "Out of line with what? What's really bothering you?" "Well," he said, "they're making more money than I am." That's the way we finally got to the heart of the matter! And, you know, shortly after I left the company, the president bought back all the contracts of the district managers—at a fantastic cost. But, at least, they didn't make more money than he did after that.

These two case histories have made me realize that if a company truly wants greatly increased sales and profit, it must be willing to put its money where its mouth is and pay an accelerating sales commission, which gives the salesman an increasingly higher percentage of the extra sales he obtains. And if the salesman occasionally makes more than his boss, so be it. It may make him want to continue as an outstanding salesman, rather than become a poor manager.

For one thing, if such an approach is not adopted, the outstanding salesman will receive little more than the mediocre salesman because of the inertia effect of the base salary. Let me illustrate. Salesman A has a base salary of $10,000 per year and he earns a 5 percent commission on his sales of $200,000. His commission earnings are therefore $10,000, and his total compensation is $20,000. Salesman B also earns a base salary of $10,000 per year, but he sells $400,000 per year at the same 5 percent commission rate. Thus his commission earnings are $20,000, and his total compensation is $30,000. Now, Salesman B earns twice as much commission as Salesman A because he sold twice as much, but his total compensation has increased by only 50 percent because of the inertia effects of the base salary. If, as in many companies, the commission rate were actually decelerating—say, 5 percent on the first $200,000 of sales and 2.5 percent on the next $200,000—Salesman B's compensation would be only 25 percent higher than Salesman A's.

What with some companies' practice of paying a smaller and smaller share of increased sales and the federal government's practice of taking a larger and larger share of increased earnings, there isn't much incentive left for a man to produce greater results.

Another subject of great interest to me is executive bonus plans.

The first question that is always raised in designing an executive bonus plan is, How many people should be included in the plan? I don't believe there is any magic number that fits every company. I do believe, however, that participation in the plan should be restricted to those managers who have a substantial impact on profits. Generally speaking, the correct number tends to work out at around one percent of the company's total population. For example, if the company has 30,000 employees, about 300 managers would typically be eligible for the bonus plan. But the number varies —and rightfully so—depending on how the company is organized and the type of industry in which it is engaged. For example, a highly centralized company is likely to need considerably fewer bonus participants than one which is highly decentralized and has a number of managers making important decisions. A highly capital-intensive company also tends to need fewer bonus participants than one which is highly labor-intensive.

The next question that arises in designing a bonus plan is, What level of awards should be paid? Most companies generate a pool of bonus money by applying a preestablished formula to the profit and loss statement and balance sheet. When I was at one company, we followed the same basic approach. I met with the managers on my team and asked them to help me design a valid and adequate bonus formula. My feeling was that the salary a manager receives is payment for at least minimal results and that a bonus plan shouldn't start generating any funds until those minimum results have been achieved. So I asked my team, "How much profit are you willing to give me as payment for your salaries?" After some discussion, we agreed that we ought to deliver enough profit to pay the interest on the bonds, the dividends on the preferred stock, and a reasonable dividend on the common stock before we earned any incentive awards. We also decided that this profit level should be stated in terms of return on investment, because, after all, that was the reason we were in business.

These minimum profit levels translated into an 8 percent return on investment before provision for income taxes. That sort of return was nothing to write home about, and most companies were surpassing it routinely, but it was designed to represent only the minimum acceptable performance below which no bonuses would be paid.

We then built our incentive fund on profits which were in excess of this 8 percent pretax return on investment. We decided that each full participant would get 2 percent of his salary for each one-point return above 8 percent. Therefore, at a 13 percent pretax return, each full participant would get a bonus equal to 10 percent of his salary. That wasn't much of a bonus, but then 13 percent wasn't much of a pretax return on investment either.

We went on to decide that we would pay 3 percent of salary for each one-point return above 13 percent but below 26 percent pretax return on investment and 4 percent for each one-point return above 26 percent.

Now, this type of formula is steeply accelerated. Like the right type of sales incentive compensation formula, it provides a tangible incentive to the company's managers to get out and improve the profits. It also implicitly recognizes that the two-point improvement between a 26 and a 28 percent return on investment is one hell of a lot harder to attain than the two points between 9 percent and 11 percent. It's a lot easier to come up to average if you are lousy than it is to become superb if you are already damn good.

Our bonus plan at this company worked out beautifully, and in some years executives were receiving bonuses equal to 100 percent of their salaries. I might add that the stockholders received an even bigger return than the executives.

The third question in bonus plan design is, How should you distribute the bonus money?

Well, we assigned each participant a weight based on his salary level. Those at the bottom were weighted *1;* those in the middle were weighted *2;* and those at the top management levels were weighted *3.* Except for this weighting according to salary level, the bonuses were prorated to salary. The weighting, of course, gave the top management executives as a group a percentage bonus which was three times that of the lowest-paid participants. Such an approach reflected the fact that the higher the level of management, the greater was the potential contribution to profits—or losses, for that matter.

Now, many managers will disagree with my group incentive approach. They maintain that awards from the bonus plan should be distributed on a discretionary basis, according to the individual's personal performance for the year. Under that alternative, some executives would get huge bonuses and some would get no bonuses. I have had some pressure for this approach even within the companies I have run. A case history will demonstrate the reason I favor group incentives rather than individual incentives.

At one company we had eight profit centers, but the amount of profits that were generated by each profit center differed widely. One division manager's profit center made more money than all the other seven put together. One day he came to me and said, "Don, your group incentive approach isn't fair. My team is making fabulous profits, and that division manager over in Rochester is losing money. Yet we all get the same percentage of bonus."

Well, I knew that my "fabulously profitable" division manager could have made the same profits if he had sat home and watched television each year—

maybe more profits, now that I come to think of it! He was in a business which was booming, and we were the industry leaders. I also knew that my division manager in Rochester was working four times as hard as the other man just to keep the losses down to a reasonable level. He was in a fledgling business that was in the early part of its growth cycle. Some day, his hour was bound to come, but not without a tremendous amount of effort.

So I said to my fabulously successful division manager, "It's obvious from your profit and loss statement that you have some really excellent people on your team. Since we're on a group incentive basis, why don't you lend several of your team members to the division manager in Rochester? With their help, the Rochester operation can undoubtedly move from a loss to a profit position, and your bonus therefore will improve also." I said this, I must admit, with the full knowledge that this division manager would never adopt such a course of action. It had its intended effect, however, because he left my office and I didn't hear from him again for a year.

He then reappeared with the same old argument. "My profits are still fantastic and that guy in Rochester is still losing money. It just isn't fair." I replied, "Well, maybe you're right. I've been thinking things over, and perhaps a more equitable approach would be to distribute half the bonus fund on the basis of group achievement and the other half on individual achievement.

But, before I agree to such a plan, I feel I should tell you I'm thinking of sending you to Rochester to run that division." Once again my division manager left the office, and this time I never had any more bonus suggestions from him!

Actually, I could be persuaded that a combination of group and individual incentive bonuses might be somewhat better than total group bonuses or total individual bonuses, although I am frankly concerned about most managers' ability to assess the performance of their team members in an accurate and equitable manner. I think the job can be done, but many managers have neither the time nor the guts to do the job right. And, if individual awards are not established on a fair basis, the organization is in for more trouble than would be encountered with virtually any other bonus distribution system. I have seen groups of executives demoralized by what they regarded as capricious handling of bonus funds. Charges of "fair-haired boy" were rampant around the company.

Whatever the system, however, I feel that it must contain a healthy element of group incentive. Certainly, a company wants to encourage individual initiative; but, more important, it must encourage teamwork. Throughout this book, I have repeatedly used the phrase "management team." That choice of words has not been made lightly, for I feel that the essence of good management is teamwork in accomplishing a common goal. I once attended a football game where the star gained 230 yards in rushing, and yet the team lost 50 to 0. Now, the star may get a fabulous offer from the pros, but the team isn't likely to make it to the Rose Bowl.

The result of using a totally discretionary bonus system in some companies I have seen is an organization which bears more than a passing resemblance to the Metropolitan Opera. Like the stars at the Met, executives at these companies posture grandly before anyone who will watch, hog the spotlight from their fellow executives, and refuse to "sing" if the conditions are not exactly to their liking. The president plays the role of Rudolph Bing, and he is just about as frustrated.

My experience with the Metropolitan Opera is that some performances are utterly magnificent, and others are deplorable. That, I believe, is the product of the star system. Business cannot afford to operate that way, however. From the stockholders' point of view as well as that of the employees, a succession of small but steady increases in profits and earnings per share is far preferable to magnificence one year and virtual bankruptcy the next.

There is another point that should be made concerning bonus plans. In most companies, it is the president who makes the final decision as to bonus participants and the amount of award they will receive (if there is an individual element to the plan). There is nothing undesirable in this procedure, because the president can look across the entire company and insure that a reasonable degree of equity is achieved. Besides, only he knows exactly how much money is in the pot.

However, I have seen countless companies where the president, and not the participants' own supervisor, breaks the good news concerning a bonus award. Ostensibly, the reason for this approach is to keep bonus amounts highly secret and to make the participant feel that his contributions are personally appreciated by the president himself. Frankly, I feel that the real reason for such an approach is to give the president a chance to play Santa Claus. The usual result is that the participant goes to his supervisor to thank him for granting him an award, and the supervisor replies, "Oh, did you get an award? How much was it?" It is no wonder that some participants begin to "end run" their obviously powerless supervisors and look to someone higher up in the management hierarchy for their rewards.

A practice which a number of companies have adopted or are considering is to defer all or part of each executive's bonus and pay it out in a series of equal annual installments. These installments start after retirement in some companies, and in others they start in the year of the award, with the last installment paid four to five years later. Several reasons are offered for this approach, but the most important is that the employee is ostensibly given an incentive to remain with the company because, if he resigns, he loses any installments which have not yet been paid. This forcible deferral approach has been labeled "the golden handcuffs" method by some of its critics.

I think the critics have a point. Actually, the executive is not given an incentive to stay with the company, but a "disincentive" to leave the company. Forcible deferrals, then, are a negatively oriented motivational device, and many executives react to them in a highly negative manner. If the executive has been covered by the deferred compensation arrangements for a long enough time, it is true that he will have built up a sizable stake in the company, and another company will have to pay dearly to offset the amounts he will lose. On the other hand, executives who have been covered by such arrangements for only a few years are made more vulnerable to the blandishments of another company, because their actual cash flow compensation is substantially less than their nominal compensation. For example, take a man who is earning $30,000 per year in salary. He receives a $15,000 bonus which is paid to him in five equal annual installments. In the first year of such an arrangement, he therefore receives a total of $33,000. It will not be until five such bonuses have been paid that the executive will actually be receiving the $45,000 per year that the company says he is earning. During that first year, therefore, the executive might find a $45,000 per year offer from a competitor very attractive—if that offer included immediate and not deferred payment.

The fact is, a company which really wants to attract someone from another company usually has no difficulty in conjuring up a compensation package to do the trick. Then, too, compensation is not the only reason that a person stays with or leaves a company, although it is probably the most important one.

I remember that in one company with which I was associated we used to employ a rule of thumb in attracting executives from our three major competitors. In the case of one competitor's executives, we knew we had to give the men more money and a higher title to get them. If we wanted someone from a second competitor, we offered the same money and the same title. The third competitor's executives were happy to come with us for less money and a lower title.

To a limited degree, I am in favor of allowing the executive certain choices as to how and when his compensation is to be paid. For example, the individual ought to be able to decide whether he wants his bonus in a lump sum immediately or in a series of installments. He ought to be able to name the number of installments he wants and the time they are to commence. If the deferred compensation is invested in company stock, he ought to be able to choose whether the dividends on such stock will be paid to him as declared or reinvested in more company stock. Of course, any deferred compensation which is chosen voluntarily in the manner I have described should be nonforfeitable. It doesn't make much sense to give the man a free choice between immediate and deferred payment, and then tell him that if he chooses the deferred route he will lose the money in the event that he quits.

Such an approach allows the individual to tailor at least part of the compensation package to his own needs. For example, he might desire to have a more stable income and therefore would find a five-year cycle of bonus payments very attractive. On the other hand, he might need as much cash as possible to send his children through college, and, in that case, immediate payment would be the method he would choose. Other executives nearing retirement would probably favor postretirement installments.

Using the logic I have described, some compensation experts have advocated going all the way and letting the individual executive make unlimited choices on each and every aspect of his total compensation package. Under such an approach, the individual could, for example, give up all or part of his group life and medical insurance or his retirement benefit and take an increased salary. I believe that this is going too far, however. I don't doubt that, given the opportunity, many younger executives would cancel their group life and medical insurance benefits, and perhaps their retirement benefits also, in order to live a little better. That is what worries me.

I suppose it may smack of paternalism, but I think that, to a limited degree at least, the company has to look out for the long-range interests of its executives and, if you will, protect some of them from themselves. Of course, those arguing for *total* individualization will say, "Let him do what he wants, and, if he loses his shirt, that's his problem—not yours." I don't think it will work out in that way, however. It *will* be the company's problem, because the executive will make it the company's problem and may even blame the company for being so imprudent as to allow him the opportunity to make such a drastic mistake.

Stock options are still very powerful compensation devices, despite the recent limitations placed on them by the 1964 Revenue Act. Under the new rules, the executive must exercise his option within five years after it is granted (instead of ten years), and he must hold the stock for at least three years after its exercise (instead of six months) to qualify for long-term capital gains tax treatment on all the appreciation which has accrued above the original option price.

Without a doubt, the government has made stock options less appealing, but the possibility of long-term capital gains tax treatment, no matter how difficult it is to attain, is always more appealing than the staggering income taxes that top executives must currently pay on their salaries and bonuses. For many executives, profits from stock options are one of the few ways to build an estate of even reasonable size.

Stock options, of course, are not an entirely fair method of compensation. While it is true that the earnings of the company are subject to the control of the executives and that the earnings of the company, over the long term, have a great influence on the market value of the company's stock, there are several other variables affecting market value over which the executives have no control whatsoever. I have seen executives in so-called defensive companies who have done a superlative job, but whose options have certain submarine-like qualities: They are under water most of the time. On the other hand, I have seen executives in so-called glamour companies, whose chief virtue consisted in being able to dream up an exotic name for their enterprise. "Synergistic Autotronics, Inc." becomes a smash hit with certain types of investors, and, even though the company loses staggering sums of money, its stock sells at a price-earnings multiple that can't even be calculated (fifty times what?). In such companies the executives' options have made them millionaires, and yet the future may show this to be an instance of gross overcompensation.

On the other side of the ledger, stock options do tend to make the stockholders and the executives of a company mutually interdependent. If the executive owns a piece of the action, he is more likely to make decisions that will protect his stake in the business. In so doing, he cannot help but benefit all the other stockholders.

Despite the limitations we have discussed, I believe that stock options can still be a valuable part of many companies' compensation packages, provided they are used intelligently. By that I mean that their use should be restricted to the top policy-making executives of a company (10 to 20 people at most). These individuals are the only ones who can influence the overall earnings of the company, and they are the ones for whom long-term capital gains tax treatment offers a considerable advantage. Middle management executives do not have sufficient influence on the *total* earnings of the company, nor do they stand to benefit that much from long-term capital gains tax treatment.

Then, too, the company pays a price to secure favorable tax treatment for the executive. It cannot deduct any income to the executive on which he pays long-term capital gains tax rates. This aspect of the tax laws makes stock options not only an inappropriate compensation device for lower-level managers but a very expensive one to boot!

I have seen a number of companies that either give no salary increase at the same time an individual is promoted or else give a very small salary increase. In the first instance, the company is holding back until "the man proves himself in his new job." In the second instance, the increase is held down because, "After all, he just received a big merit increase." To me, both of these practices are deplorable.

In selecting a man to fill a big job, you have implicitly decided that you think he can perform that job.

Why, then, is it necessary to hedge your bet and either give him the job on an acting basis or give him the job with no increase in salary until he verifies your original belief that he is a good man? My policy has always been to give the man the job, with no strings attached, and give him a sizable increase in salary at the time he takes the job, thereby furnishing him tangible evidence that I recognize the significantly increased responsibilities he is assuming. If it occasionally occurs that the man doesn't work out, I remove him; and he understands that those are the ground rules.

A person who takes on a bigger job also takes on a bigger risk. The higher one goes in any organization, the easier it is to be identified as the source of great success or great failure. As Harry Truman observed about his job as President, "The buck stops here." If the risk is greater, then the reward must also be greater, or it is going to be awfully difficult to find people to accept the higher job—unless, of course, they are confirmed masochists.

In my opinion, companies structure their compensation systems to make people really want to take those higher jobs, with their higher risks. One way to do this is to grant large salary increases for promotions. The fact that the individual just received a merit increase is, to me, immaterial. I can't get concerned even if the individual doubles his salary in one year through a combination of merit and promotional increases. I know that some people say, "You'll spoil him if you

give him too much money within such a short period."
There is always that risk, but there is an even greater
risk that you will lose him if you don't give him the
money he deserves.

I consider titles to be related to compensation, if
not actually another element of compensation. The
problem of establishing proper and equitable titles gives
most companies fits.

Titles have come to be a shorthand way of assessing
the worth of an individual. As such, they are invested
with considerable status. I remember hearing a story
concerning S. Clark Beise, formerly of the Bank of
America. Mr. Beise was at a cocktail party and started
to converse with another guest whom he had never
met. After exchanging the usual pleasantries, the other
guest got down to business. "What line of work are you
in?" he asked.

Beise replied, "I'm in banking."

"Oh, that's very interesting. And what bank do you
work for?"

"The Bank of America."

"Well, that certainly is a huge bank—the biggest in
the world, I'm told. And what do you do for the Bank
of America?"

Beise answered, "They call me President."

You may be the director of sales of a division of
IBM. And that division may itself be bigger than most
companies in the United States. Yet the customer you

visit may be more impressed with one of your smaller competitors that had the sagacity to send in its vice-president of sales to make the sales pitch. "If IBM really wanted my business," the customer may reason, "the least it could have done was send in its VP and not that ribbon clerk." The problem is, you *are* the "VP" for sales but your customer doesn't know it.

Some corporation presidents I know refuse to call their division heads president. At least one had the honesty to admit his reason: "I want there to be only one president in this place—and that's me." So Mr. C, who heads his division and carries the title vice-president—XYZ division, visits a potentially key customer. As he is leaving, the customer says, "It certainly was a pleasure to talk with you. I'd love to meet the president of your division someday."

These examples point up the fact that titles are relative. If your competitors are using vice-president titles or division president titles, you should too. You won't find very many banks that don't have just about as many vice-presidents as clerks. That may be overdoing it, but no one bank is likely to give its competitors an edge by permitting an ordinary "manager" to talk with a customer, when its competition provides him nothing but vice-presidents.

You may even want to consider getting the jump on your competition, because titles really are cheap. For that matter, so is a private office with a carpet. Of course, there is always the executive who will tell you,

"I don't care what they call me, and it doesn't matter whether my office floor is covered with carpeting or concrete. It's what I take home in that little pay envelope that counts." Have you ever noticed that most executives who deliver such speeches usually do so in a plushly carpeted office from behind a desk that could comfortably seat 40 for dinner? If you can read backward, you will also notice a title on the door which in length and superlatives rivals those that were assigned to Suleiman the Magnificent.

Status is alive and well in American business, and don't let anyone tell you differently.

X

The Corporate Staff

A president's staff can be of tremendous value to him, provided it is correctly used.

There are two basic roles that a staff man plays. The first is as an expert in his field. If he is a personnel man, he must know more about industrial relations than anyone else in his company—and, if possible, more than anyone else in any other company as well. If he is the controller, he must know more about financial management than anyone else in his company.

The second role of a staff man is to be the eyes and ears of the president inside the company and to be his personal representative.

In his role as expert, the staff man prepares various policy statements and directives to insure that all parts of the organization are working together to achieve common objectives. He does not command these policies into being. He sells the president on their virtues, and the president orders their implementation.

The staff man also provides his expertise to line managers. But he does this on an advisory basis. The line manager may not take the staff man's advice, and, if the latter feels strongly enough about it, he may appeal his case to the president, who in turn may order that the line manager adopt a certain course of action. But, again, it is the president and not the staff man who issues the orders.

The staff man must be a supersalesman. Like any good salesman, he must know his product thoroughly, and it must be clear to his customer that he does. He must be able to package a sales pitch for his product which emphasizes the particular advantages that the customer is seeking. He must know how to close a sale. Although many staff men would rebel at the thought, the old sales dictum, "The customer is always right," has its place in the world of staff–line relationships.

This describes the way in which I think a staff man, in his role as expert, should operate. It is not how staff men in some companies *do* operate, however.

First of all, staff men in some companies give orders. The vice-president of personnel refuses to approve an increase for a manager in the engineering department. In effect, he has ordered the vice-president of engineering not to give his subordinate an increase. The vice-president of engineering thinks to himself (and sometimes out loud), "Just who is running this department anyway? Me or the personnel guy?" It is an appropriate question. The vice-president of personnel should never be given the authority to countermand some other executive's actions. If he feels so strongly that the vice-president of engineering is out of his mind, he can always take his case to the president for final adjudication.

Suppose you set out to buy a new car. You visit Dealer A, listen to the pitch by one of the salesmen, test-drive the car, and then decide it isn't quite right for you. So you call it a day and decide to look again next week. Three days later, your wife receives a letter from the car salesman: "Dear Madam, I just wanted you to know how stupid your husband is. He obviously knows nothing about fine automobiles or he would have had the sense to buy my product!"

Well, that's the way some staff men seem to operate. If they can't sell their product on its merits, they go back to the home office and let the president know what an idiot he has for a division general manager.

Let me continue my analogy. You go out once again to look for a new car, and this time you visit Dealer B. After listening to the sales pitch and test-driving the car, you decide that this is the automobile for you. So you sign the papers and the salesman promises delivery in two days. Within minutes of leaving the showroom, you are congratulating yourself on your taste in picking out fine automobiles and on the deal you just consummated. The salesman is completely forgotten. When you pick up the car a few days later, you find painted across the doors on both sides the legend: "This car was sold by Joe Smith."

There are staff men in some companies who are like Joe Smith. They sell their product but they refuse to give their customers any credit for buying it. "After all," they reason, "anybody with the slightest amount of intelligence can see that my way is the *only* way." In one form or another, they see to it that the product they sell bears the legend: "Sold by Joe Smith."

Small wonder that many line managers resent any intrusion of staff men into their affairs. I can remember one division general manager in California who refused to let a certain staff man through the gate of his plant. Heated telephone conversations took place between New York and California, and soon the staff man found himself on a plane headed back to New York. He never did get his job done.

Of course, I must admit that there are some line managers who exhibit paranoid feelings toward staff men and, like true paranoids, have no basis in reality for these feelings. This is a problem to be handled by the president of the company.

So how should a staff man operate to gain his objectives? Like the salesman he is, I believe it is vitally important for a staff man to make his customer look good. In one company, we had an internal auditor who was great on the numbers, but never seemed to get his recommendations implemented. He would visit a division, spend a few weeks sniffing around, and then come home and write a report. The report was given only to the president. After reading it, the president would telephone his division manager. "What in God's name is going on out there? John (the internal auditor) says your systems and procedures are deplorable." Naturally, the division manager reacts defensively. Even though he knows himself that his current systems are deplorable, he is going to fight for them because he has been attacked personally.

Some time later, we replaced this internal auditor with a new man. His approach was considerably different. He would go to a division and also spend some time sniffing around. He would then return to the home office and write his report. But his next step—and here is where he differed from the first internal auditor—was to go back out to the division and meet with the division manager. He would discuss the findings, conclusions, and recommendations in his report in a nonjudgmental way. Usually, the division manager would say, "I know about these deficiencies, and I am in the process of correcting them." Well, the probability is that the division manager really doesn't know very much at all about the problems the internal auditor uncovered, but he isn't going to admit it. And he is going to correct them before the old man jumps down his throat.

The internal auditor returns once again to the home office and submits his report to the president. This time he adds to his report the observation, "The division manager is aware of these problems and has indicated that he is in the process of correcting them." The division manager is a hero. The internal auditor doesn't get quite the glory that he otherwise might, but, more importantly, he gets the job done. Moreover, his advice is thereafter likely to be solicited actively by that division manager he helped.

In dealing with my corporate staff members, I have always insisted on what the army calls "completed staff work." Occasionally (but usually only once), a staff man would come to me and say, "Now, we can handle this problem in one of three ways. What do you think?" I would show him the door unceremoniously and leave with him the thought that "I am paid to make decisions. You are paid to think."

I expect a staff man to identify all the alternative courses of action and to analyze each as to its advantages and disadvantages. Finally, I expect him to come to me and present his findings and conclusions together with specific recommendations as to why one of the alternatives should be adopted over the others. All I have left to do at that point is to say "go" or "stop."

At the beginning of this chapter, I mentioned that a key role of corporate staff personnel is to act as the eyes and ears of the president and as his personal representative. This is a role that is often overlooked by company presidents.

When the president shows up at the plant in Tuscaloosa, he immediately creates a big stir, whether he is there just to visit or to hold an important meeting, whether he makes a speech to the employees or says not a word. The word spreads through the plant like wildfire: "The old man's here. Something must be up."

If the president merely wants to find out what is going on at the Tuscaloosa plant, why not send in his vice-president of personnel? This action will establish a pattern of mobility around the company so that, when the vice-president shows up, not one eyebrow will be raised. He can take the plant personnel manager aside and, in a very informal way, find out what the president wants to know.

The president can also use staff men to bounce some of his ideas off his line executives, without the line managers knowing that the ideas emanated from him. In that way, he can get some objective appraisals rather than self-serving acceptance.

How big should the corporate staff be? The answer to this question is dependent on the company's type of organization. In a centralized organization, the corporate staff is the entire staff. In a decentralized organization with profit-responsible divisions, the corporate staff should be held to a minimum and each division should have its own staff as soon as it is large enough to support it. Division staff members should report to the division manager and not to their corporate staff counterparts. I don't mind seeing the so-called dotted line between, say, a corporate vice-president of marketing and a division vice-president of marketing, but the line should always remain dotted. There is sometimes a tendency for the corporate staff man to fill in the white spaces between the dots—one at a time—until one day he, not the division manager, is the division staff man's real *boss*.

Corporate staffs operate in accordance with Parkinson's law. No matter how large they grow, everyone always seems to be busy. The larger the corporate staff, the more likely it is to begin interfering in decisions which have been delegated to the line managers. I think it is also always appropriate to say that the larger the corporate staff, the less the overall caliber of its personnel. To rephrase Malthus's law, as the corporate staff grows geometrically, the number of experts on it grows only arithmetically—if that. I want all—not just some—of my staff people to be top-flight experts.

XI

The President's Job

*W*ith but few exceptions, the president's job is no different from any other manager's. He has to formulate goals so he knows where he is going. He has to make his team believe that he knows where he is going. And he has to follow the same management fundamentals as other managers in leading his team to the attainment of these goals.

To me, the president can have only one job, and that is to be chief executive of the company. Now, that statement may trouble certain board chairmen who have retained the chief executive's title for themselves. Such a development has usually arisen because the current chairman formerly was the president and chief executive officer. When he moved to the chairman's job, he took his chief executive's title with him. Now, there may have been a perfectly valid reason for such an approach, because the new president did not have enough experience to immediately assume the chief executive's role. But that reason is valid only for six months to a year at most, because if the president isn't ready to be chief executive within that time period he will probably never be ready, and therefore he should be replaced.

Why is it, then, that some chairmen keep their chief executive titles for years—right up to their retirement? Personally, I think one reason is that they don't want to let go the reins of power.

As I see it, the chairman's job is to guide the board of directors and, if he was formerly president, to act as a "senior citizen" and offer the new president the benefit of his experience. The president's job is to run the company, to make all major policy decisions which do not require board approval, and to submit "new legislation" to the board for its consideration.

Because the jobs of these two executives are so different, I think two different individuals should hold them. I am not in favor of combining the chairman's and president's positions into one superjob. I realize that having two jobs increases the payroll costs a bit, but the results that can be achieved by two men, each doing his own "thing," is well worth the cost.

For much the same reasons, I am absolutely against the president's handling a job on his team on an acting basis. Often this development occurs when a vice-president moves up to president and just can't bear to give up his former job. He rationalizes, "I'll handle it just a little longer and in the meantime look for a top qualified replacement." To his immense relief, he never seems to be able to find quite the right man, and so he keeps the job until the pressures of his presidency force him to give it up.

Not too many years ago, some baseball teams used to have player-managers. The individual managed the team and at the same time played first base. It seems there was a distinct tendency for the other members of the team to throw the ball to first base, even if the runner was approaching third! You can't exactly blame them. They sure made the boss look good. For the same reason, I think the president should have only one job and should never take a job on his own team.

A widely heralded recent development is to create what is known as the "president's office." In this type of organization, three or four executives report to the president and they are all shown in the same organizational box with the president. All the other top managers report to *everyone* in the box. This form of organization, it is said, takes a tremendous load off the president. It may, temporarily, but in my opinion it is an undesirable way to run a company.

If you study a number of companies with president's offices, you will find that they evolved in much the same way. A long time ago the company was centralized. There were vice-presidents of engineering, manufacturing, sales, personnel, and so on, and they all reported to the president. As the business grew, the pres-

ident saw fit to delegate more and more of his responsibilities, until one day he established a number of profit-
responsible divisions. The business kept growing and
so did the number of divisions, until the president had
20 division managers reporting to him in addition to his
corporate staff. So he created some group vice-presidents. Each was given responsibility for several divisions. But the business grew still more, and pretty soon
the president had ten group vice-presidents plus his
corporate staff reporting to him.

At that point he thought to himself, "What I need is
an executive vice-president to assist me. But no matter
where I place him my group vice-presidents are going
to think I have selected a crown prince. All but the one
I select is going to be very unhappy, and I may lose
them to my competitors." So he opened a president's
office and staffed it with three or four men (sometimes
more). Now there are still some unhappy group vice-
presidents but not as many as there would have been
had only one executive vice-president been chosen.

I believe that only one man can be held responsible
for carrying out a given activity. It is almost impossible
to blame a committee when something goes wrong.
And that is what the office of the president can end up
being.

Furthermore, I think that a man should have only
one boss. In the office-of-the-president form of organization, the managers reporting to the people in that
crowded box have three or four bosses. Surely, at times

they could get three different decisions on a given subject, depending on which of their bosses they approached. Yet, if the president's office had to act in concert, much time would be lost while waiting for the august group to begin its deliberations.

History has taught that a duumvirate, a triumvirate, or any other "umvirate" is an inherently unstable combination. The minute such a power structure is formed, its members begin to jockey for position. The same will probably happen within the president's office. Over a period of time, a definite successor to the president will emerge from the pack and, whether or not he is formally designated as such, everyone will know it. At that point, the office of the president will be in its death throes.

From time to time, articles appear in *The Wall Street Journal* or *Business Week* which list all the horrors of the president's job: his tendency to get ulcers and heart attacks; the terrible pressure he is under. My experience, however, is that a good part of the pressure is self-made.

Many presidents never seem to have time to make use of the management fundamentals we have been discussing. They aren't able to delegate responsibility and decision making to subordinates because they are too busy putting out fires. They operate from crisis to crisis, and it is a miracle that such men don't get ulcers and heart attacks more often than they do.

More than any other manager, it is vital that the president delegate because he has more responsibilities than any other manager.

Now, this is not to say that, after the president makes full use of all the management fundamentals, his job becomes a snap. He must still bear ultimate responsibility for the success of the company. That responsibility *cannot* be delegated. As a result, the president's job is a lonely one. But it need not be all that stressful.

The president has certain responsibilities which are peculiar to his particular position. The first of these is the necessity to deal with Wall Street.

It is my view that the president should handle the company's major relationships with investment bankers, brokerage houses, and the like. He shouldn't delegate this responsibility to his financial vice-president, although the latter should play a part and get to know the people in the investment banking community.

In his dealings with this community the president should always be honest, presenting only the straight facts as he knows them. If for some reason he feels that he cannot divulge certain information fully and truthfully, then he should say nothing.

Similarly, in his estimates of the company's future performance the president should also try to present an accurate picture of what he thinks the company will do —not what he would like the company to do. Wall Street does not appreciate a president who predicts a glamorous future when in reality the company is about to fall on its face. Nor does Wall Street appreciate a president who is ultraconservative and ends up with earnings per share of $1.50 when he predicted only $1.

The president should—although many don't—take the advice of his investment bankers when it comes to raising additional capital. These people have devoted their careers to finance. They are the experts; the president rarely is. He may consider it quite a triumph when he succeeds in getting the rate on a bond issue shaved by 0.125 percent. But if the bonds sell below par—as his investment bankers probably predicted—he really has gained nothing.

The president, however, must establish the company's basic approach to the generation of new capital. Should the company go into debt? Should it issue more common stock? Preferred stock? Convertible debentures? It is the president who must finally approve the recommendations that are made to the board of directors.

Another task of the president is to formulate a dividend policy and sell it to the board of directors. In so doing, he must consider that there is going to be a good deal of inertia attached to whatever is decided. It is no accident that companies which pay a high proportion of their earnings as dividends attract stockholders who want large dividends. Conversely, so-called growth companies which pay no dividends and plow all their earnings back into the business tend to attract stock-holders looking for capital gains appreciation. So, in formulating a dividend policy, the president must look down the road and make his recommendation with the future (not merely the current year) in mind. Some companies have begun to "individualize" dividend policies by issuing participating preferred stock which permits the individual investor to shoot for capital gains, maximum dividends, or any combination in between in accordance with his personal needs.

I frequently address groups of high school and college students who are considering a career in business, and one of the questions I am often asked is, "How do you get to be president of a company?"

First of all, let me say what you don't have to be to be president. You don't have to be a "hail fellow," a back-slapping extrovert. I have met many successful presidents who were really rather withdrawn, introspective individuals.

You don't have to look like Gregory Peck or Rock Hudson. Not many presidents do.

You don't have to be a marvelous speaker, although it helps. I have known excellent presidents who gave speeches only when they were up against the wall.

You don't have to be a genius. There are very few geniuses in the world and—thank God—very few idiots either.

What, then, *do* you have to do to become president? First, you must be reasonably intelligent—somewhere in the range between genius and idiot.

You must be a good manager. You must know how to apply management fundamentals.

You must be willing to make decisions—dirty decisions, where you could go either way and you won't know whether you are right for several years. In other words, you must have guts.

You must really want to be president and must be willing to sacrifice the time and effort required to reach your goal.

You must perform every job you are assigned better than the person who held it before you.

My young audiences take this all in, but, still not satisfied, they ask more questions.

"Isn't the competition brutal as you near the top?" Frankly, I think that the higher you go, the easier it gets. I remember one president telling me, "The competition is greatest at the lower levels; there is always room at the top." I believe he was right, for success seems to breed more of the same. The trick is to get one's head above the crowd. Of course, there is always the risk that it will be shot off, but people who fear such risks shouldn't aim for the presidency in the first place.

"What is the best educational preparation to be president?" People from every imaginable educational background have become president. However, I think one's chances are increased with an undergraduate degree in liberal arts and a graduate degree in business administration. If only an undergraduate degree is to be obtained, I prefer liberal arts to business because the former gives the individual a broader outlook, and the latter is not of sufficient depth to be rewarding.

"Which discipline offers the best road to the top?" The answer to that question is partially dependent on the particular problems business is encountering at any given point in time. I remember that marketing men were the fair-haired boys during the depression, when the trick was to get the stuff sold. Right after World War II, when the demand for goods far exceeded the supply, production men came into their glory. Now, in the age of conglomerates and more decentralized organizations, it is the financial man who appears to have the inside track. I do think, however, that the presidential aspirant should concentrate his efforts in marketing, production, or finance. A possible exception is engineering, especially where the company is engaged in highly technical fields. Experience in other disciplines, although valuable, is far less likely to lead to the presidency of a company.

"Is it better to stay in one discipline, or should one seek as much rotation as possible?" Many people will disagree with me, but I favor remaining with one discipline and riding it to the top. If the company employs operations review meetings such as I have described earlier, a manager can gain, over a period of time, a considerable amount of knowledge in other disciplines just by listening carefully to the presentations that are being made and the problems that are being discussed. Of course, I would not hesitate to change disciplines if requested to do so.

"Should one stay with a single company or change jobs every so often?" I know I'm going to get considerable disagreement on my answer to this question, but I believe there is much to be gained from a series of employment changes. The individual cannot help but broaden his experience—and his contacts. Having to learn new ways of doing things, absorb new philosophies, and meet new people makes the person more flexible and more easily able to tolerate change. And change is what the president's job is all about.

One of the most important attributes that a good president must have is knowing when to step down. On that score I have seen a regrettably high number of presidents fail. Ever since they joined the company, they have known that 65 was the mandatory retirement age. But here they are at 64½, and they still haven't planned for an orderly succession. If you ask them why, they will answer, "I've been so busy running the company that I just haven't had the time to groom anybody to succeed me." Hogwash! Part of the job of running the company is to provide for its future—and that means preparing the next president. Frankly, I think the real reason these presidents don't groom a successor until the last moment is their belief that, with so little preparation, there is a better chance that their successor will fail miserably. The odds are certainly with them. And, should that happen, they have a fantasy in the back of their mind that the board of directors will make an exception from the mandatory retirement age and ask them—better yet, beg them—to stay and save the company.

When presidents of this type are finally forced out of the company, they usually don't live very long thereafter because, just as they didn't prepare for a successor, they also didn't prepare for what to do subsequent to their retirement. So they read for a week, garden for a week, fish for another week, and generally get under their wives' feet. (One wife told me, "I married him for better or for worse—but not for lunch.") By and by, when they can't find anything better to do, they die.

When I was in college, I read a book entitled *A Dutch Boy 50 Years Later*, by Edward Bok, who suggested that one's life ought to be divided into three parts. The first part should be preparation; the second part should be attainment; and the third part should be repayment. By repayment, the author meant providing society a return on its investment in you. This book had a great impact on me, and I decided right then and there to set up such a plan of life for myself. I immediately discovered that it is difficult to divide one's life in thirds when one isn't sure how long that life is going to be. Well, I decided that 75 years was a reasonable expectation—at least according to the actuarial tables. I then allowed myself the first 25 years for the preparation phase. However, I thought 25 years was a little too short for the attainment phase, so I upped it to 30. I therefore concluded that I should retire at age 55 and devote whatever years I had left to the repayment phase.

My life plan has worked out pretty well so far. I actually retired at 57, but had I not planned to retire at age 55 I would probably still be trying to hang on to my job. My skills and abilities led me to concentrate my repayment phase on lecturing to management people and students and sitting on the boards of a number of companies, where I could be of service to younger executives.

Other retired executives can profitably spend their time teaching in universities, serving with hospitals, sitting on school boards, and the like. These people have a great deal of experience, and most of them are not only willing but eager to share it with others and thereby repay their debt to society. Anything is better than doing only gardening and fishing!

When I was around 52 I decided that, if I was going to retire at 55 according to my life plan, I had better begin preparing a successor. There was at that time only one obvious choice for the job, and so I made my production vice-president an executive vice-president with the idea that he would become president

within a year. I made a fundamental mistake, however.
I didn't really train him for the presidency. I assumed
that he would learn the job himself through some mystical, osmotic process. Well, he hung on to his job as
production vice-president and wouldn't let go. (Of
course, a new production vice-president had been chosen, but that didn't stop him.) And he never learned
how to be president.

Meanwhile, without really knowing it, I continued
to assume all the duties of the presidency. So, when he
was elected president, he knew no more about the job
than he did the day he became executive vice-president. Thinking otherwise, I relinquished to him all my
responsibilities as chief executive officer. He foundered,
and in eighteen months he died. To this day, I don't
think he had to die. But he was hopelessly lost in his
job and thought his failure was entirely his own fault.
Yet it was I who in many ways had failed him by not
properly training him for his new and far greater responsibilities.

No man is automatically ready for the presidency of
a company—even if he was the best marketing man in
the world or the best production man. He must be
trained to be an effective president. This requires that
he be designated the new president—either implicitly
or explicitly. My usual approach has been to designate
my successor executive vice-president and make him a
member of the board of directors. I don't have to make

a formal announcement to the other team members who lost out in the competition. They know—and telling them only rubs salt in their wounds.

Once a successor is established, he should be given a steadily increasing diet of the president's responsibilities so that one day, in a relatively painless manner, he finds that he *is* the president because he is doing the president's job. Formal election can then verify this fact. It is at this point that I feel the current president, when he moves to chairman, should relinquish his chief executive officer's title to the new president.

I recognize that some people believe a new president should be named out of the blue to avoid antagonizing the inevitable losers. I can't agree with this approach because, sooner or later, the losers are going to know they have lost. By delaying this knowledge, all that has been gained is a little time. What has been lost, however, is an opportunity to train the new president and give him a good start in his new job.

XII

The Board of Directors

Some company presidents see their boards of directors as their personal Calvary. They realize the law requires that they have a board of directors, but to them the whole experience is a painful nuisance.

The viewpoint of these company presidents is unfortunate, because a board of directors can be of real service to a company.

First of all, let us consider the reason for a board's existence. According to the law, the board is elected to represent the stockholders—all of them. To my way of thinking, this means that just because a person owns 100,000 shares in the company, he is not automatically entitled to sit on the board. We do not limit congressional and senatorial posts to the country's biggest landowners and most wealthy people. The individual who owns 100,000 shares is entitled to 100,000 votes—and nothing else.

The primary responsibility of the board is to hire the most able chief executive it can find and then see that he does his job. The board doesn't run the company; it sees that the chief executive runs it.

Far from regarding a board of directors as an unnecessary nuisance, I would have had to invent a board if there had been no legal requirement to have one. For I have found that a board, properly selected, can be a marvelous source of advice and counsel. You see, I regard the board members not as adversaries but as friends. The quality of advice that one can get from his board often could not be bought at any price. Yet it is somewhat paradoxical that this advice will come at a very inexpensive price.

Who should be on the board of directors? In starting to answer this question, it is easier to state who should *not* be on the board. I do not believe in so-called inside boards comprised wholly or predominantly of company executives, with a few innocuous outside directors added for "window dressing."

An inside board is very much like a dictatorship. The president reports to the chairman. He hold meetings with the chairman when he is shaving every morning, for he is also the chairman. The board members, who are vice-presidents of the company, report to the chairman, but they also report to the president, who is also the chairman. It is all very confusing and designed to ratify whatever the president/chairman thinks should be done.

158

Now, this is not to say that the board shouldn't have some insiders on it. Of course, the chairman is automatically a member of the board, and, for all practical purposes, so is the president. In my opinion, these are the only two insiders who should be members of the board, with the exception of an executive vice-president who is being groomed for the presidency. Thus the normal number of inside directors is two, and during transition periods the number increases to three.

Now, some company presidents would disagree with this point of view. They say, "We ought to have two or three vice-presidents on the board so that the outside members will get to know them. And we also ought to have the general counsel sit on the board to furnish legal advice." This is nonsense. If a president wants his board to get to know some of his vice-presidents, all he has to do is invite them to some of the meetings to make presentations. They don't have to be members of the board.

As for the general counsel, the very reason advanced for placing him on the board (to give legal advice) is the very reason for *not* putting him on the board. The board sits to render business judgments, not legal judgments. There is in my mind a definite conflict of interest when the general counsel is a board member. When he speaks for or against a given issue, is he rendering a business judgment or a legal judgment? It isn't always easy to tell—and that is the way some general counsels seem to prefer it. The general counsel can

159

attend all the board meetings to keep the board on the legal track, but he should not be a member of the board (and that applies to one's outside counsel also).

What sort of outside members should the board contain? In three words, *the very best*. If you are the chief executive of a company making consumer products, try to get a board member who is an expert in retailing. If you are in the transportation business, get a board member who really knows the field of transportation. At one company where I am a director, the board was fortunate to obtain as a fellow director a professor of transportation at Columbia University. He has more knowledge of the transportation industry than anyone else I have ever met, and he is a most valuable board member.

People of this caliber can be a tremendous source of advice and comfort to you, the chief executive. You can't share your problems with your subordinates. You can share your problems with your wife, but you won't get much specific help. In short, you're pretty much on your own. But you can turn to the members of your board—individually and collectively—and if you have assembled a group of experts you will get the best kind of advice.

One outside director on many a company's board is the company's investment banker. Personally, I don't think he should be on the board, because his presence makes it very difficult not to give him all the investment banking business of the company. (Of course, that is precisely why so many investment bankers sit on so many boards!) On occasion, the company may be able to obtain a better deal through another investment banker, and thus a conflict-of-interest situation is bound to be created. I don't feel quite so strongly, however, about the company's commercial banker. Here, there is a greater stability of relationships, because companies change commercial bankers much less often than they do investment bankers. Your commercial banker can be a valuable source of financial advice.

Except in banks, I believe in relatively small boards. Banks, of course, elect to their boards prominent members of the community—individuals with large or potentially large accounts. They often have boards of 25 or 30 members, and the reasons for such a large board are fundamentally sound.

For other types of business, however, I believe that a board composed of 7 to 11 outside directors plus the two or three inside executives is quite ample. With a larger board, an executive committee will have to be created. Although I have served as chairman of the executive committee on occasion, I feel frankly that this committee can be abolished if the board has a relatively small membership and meets every month.

Some companies that set out to find outstanding individuals to be directors experience difficulty in signing up the people they want. I used to experience such difficulties myself until I discovered a rule that I thought applied only to executives and not to directors: If you want good men, pay them well. I believe a company that has sales of more than $200 million per year should pay its directors on the order of $10,000 annually. If the sales of the company are more than $500 million per year, the compensation should be around $15,000 annually. And when the company is in the billion-dollar class, $20,000 per year for an outstanding director is not unreasonable. These figures are merely guidelines and are intended only as an order of magnitude.

When I discuss with others my belief that directors should be well paid, someone invariably says, "Why does an individual who is probably worth millions want to sit on your board just to earn a lousy $10,000 or $20,000?" I must confess that I am not sure of the answer. All I know is that it works. I suspect that my willingness to pay a substantial fee—as directors' compensation goes—gives tangible evidence to the prospective director that I really want and need him. I am implying in effect that I am not looking for just another rubber stamp.

Moreover, many companies retire their executives at 65 but allow board members to remain until age 72. Thus a company's fee can represent a handy addition to retirement income for an executive who has reached the mandatory retirement age at his own company.

I also think that paying a substantial fee has a salutary effect on the chief executive officer. You don't get something for nothing, goes the old adage. I think it is equally true that you probably don't make too much use of something that costs you nothing—or next to nothing. That advice from world-famous medical specialists is almost invariably heeded is probably due as much to the fee that is paid for it as to the professional qualifications of the adviser.

When a substantial fee is paid, a chief executive will no longer feel guilty about bothering a director between meetings. He is paying for such advice and he expects to get it. And, I believe, the director is only too glad to give it. In fact, the more one uses one's directors, the more motivated they become. After all, the sword cuts both ways. If one pays a director a large fee and doesn't use him, the director feels guilty.

Paying a substantial fee has yet another value. It makes it easier for the chairman to ask for the director's resignation if he has outlived his purpose.

Another aid in providing for a continuous regeneration of the board is to establish a mandatory retirement age for directors. At many companies, 72 is coming to be the generally accepted retirement age. I recognize, of course, that some directors should be retired at 67 and others would still be going strong at 90—if you would let them. But the establishment of a mandatory retirement age—despite its occasional inequities—permits the resignation of board members on a more graceful and less personal basis.

XIII

Personal Financial Planning

I have stood up before many audiences of college and high school students and confidently told them, "Before you can successfully manage a business, you must first successfully manage your life." The statement had a sort of symmetry to it, and it would have made a beautiful "sampler" to be placed over the hearth.

Unfortunately, I have found literally countless cases which disprove my pious theory. Executive after executive who is renowned for his business skill and enlightened management has made a complete botch of his own personal financial affairs. Let us look at one of these executives.

He is making $50,000 per year. He has life insurance through the company which will pay $100,000 upon his death. He has some stock options, but he hasn't gotten around to exercising them yet. If he lives to age 65, he will receive a relatively modest pension from the company plus his social security benefits.

Balancing these assets are a number of liabilities. He owns a $100,000 home, but the amount of his outstanding mortage is $70,000. His principal and interest payments are around $500 per month, and with property insurance and taxes added in, his total housing costs are $700 per month. Of course, he also has utility bills, gardener's bills, garbage removal bills, and the like, and these cost him another $200 per month.

Although not technically a liability, it should be noted that our executive is sending two of his children through college at this moment, and a third is about to enter next year. He thought that he could keep his current college-education expenses constant, because at the time his third child is ready to enter college his oldest child is to graduate. But he just got a letter from "No. One Son," and, in addition to the usual request for more spending money, his pride and joy blithely dropped the bombshell that he is planning to enter medical school in the fall. So, with three children in college, our executive will have to lay out about $10,-000 per year. That amount, of course, must come out of his net income after all the taxes have been deducted.

Suppose our executive drops dead tomorrow. His wife would get the $100,000 proceeds from the insurance. Invested at 7 percent in high-grade corporate bonds, this would yield $7,000 per year, and she would still retain the principal—which, of course, is being slowly eaten away by inflation. The options could be exercised, but to do that would require some money. The borrowing costs to exercise the options would exceed the dividends on the stock and would eat into the yield on the life insurance proceeds—at least until the stock was held long enough to secure long-term capital gains tax treatment. Then it could be sold, the loan paid off (provided the stock hadn't declined in value), and the proceeds used as a source of some additional interest income.

The executive's retirement benefit turned out to be worthless, because on page 97 of the retirement booklet it says—in very small type—that the benefits are not vested in the individual until he reaches age 60—and our executive died at 57. There is of course a small social security payment.

Being as generous as we can, let's assume that after the estate has been settled and the option transaction has been handled, the executive's widow can look forward to about $10,000 per year of investment income plus her small social security benefit. Of course, the $10,000 investment income is taxable, and so she nets only $8,000.

Now, this poor widow has a few problems. Educating the children and keeping the house going take about $21,000 per year. There is also the minor problem of eating! So it appears very probable that she will have to sell the house, or stop paying for her children's education, or both.

Let's turn back the clock. All these circumstances are unchanged but our executive is still alive. We ask him, "Have you provided for your wife and family in the event of your death?"

"Of course," he answers, "I have a good-size wad of life insurance, some stock options, my company retirement benefit, and social security also. In addition, I have $30,000 equity in my house."

We continue, "Do you know what all this will add up to after your death?"

"Well," he says, "I've been meaning to sit down one Saturday and figure it all out, but I just haven't had the time. But I'm sure there's plenty for the wife and kids. The old lady and I are always joking that I'm worth more dead than alive."

How can an executive, whose whole business career is devoted to planning and organizing his company's affairs, not have the time to plan and organize his own financial affairs? Frankly, I think he didn't want to have the time, because to spend time considering whether one's wife and children will be taken care of implies that one is going to die. Now, there's a morbid thought! We plan for all sorts of contingencies—fire insurance in case the house burns down, liability insurance in case the dog bites the milkman—but we don't plan for the one of the few things in life that are not contingencies but certainties: death. Of course, we don't expect to die until we are ready. That means at about age 90 or so. And if one is going to live that long, there is plenty of time to plan for the future.

What should our "model" executive have done? What should *you* do? First, you should draw a will. Despite many people's implicit beliefs, drawing a will does not hasten your death! But someone will say, "I don't have anything to put in a will, so why bother now?" My answer to this is, "If you don't draw a will now, you will *never* have anything to put in it." A will protects your wife and children. It can help to cut down your estate taxes. And it forces you to go on and plan for your death—and for your life, too, because you really might live until you are 90.

The next thing to do is provide adequate life insurance. The key word in the last sentence is "adequate," in case you missed it. Our model executive should have had enough insurance that the income derived from the proceeds would allow his wife to keep the house, eat at least once in a while, and provide at least a little help to the children in college. In our example, "adequate" probably means around $400,000 of insurance, because the interest income on the proceeds is taxable, and we are looking for an after-tax amount.

Great cries of anguish will immediately arise from many readers who are not life insurance salesmen. "Are you out of your mind?" they will be thinking. "Life insurance is one of the worst possible investments to make." Well, I won't deny that charge, but how else

168

can you create an instant estate of $400,000 when you are still young? That is the reason life insurance should be purchased. Not until you have provided this sort of protection for your family should you feel free to indulge in some of the best possible investments.

The next thing to do is exercise your stock options as soon as possible. It's true that you may build up a bigger paper profit on the options if you wait to exercise them until just before they expire. You may, but then again you may not. And even if you do, many bad things can happen during the three-year period that the stock must be held to qualify for long-term capital gains tax treatment. Besides, are you saving the money each year so you will have it available when you do decide to exercise? Probably not. That means you will have to borrow the money, and the interest costs will eat heavily into your potential capital gains tax savings.

If you have done all these things, you are well on your way to creating a good-size estate and you have definitely assured that, no matter what happens, your wife and children will not have to suffer.

Now you can start placing some of your extra money in more promising investments. Some planning is called for here too, however.

For some reason unknown to me, there are a goodly number of executives who, although very meticulous in planning for the future in their company, follow the herd instinct in their personal investments. At lunch, one executive will say to another, "Say, I just read an interesting article on how purchasing cattle can save a lot of taxes. The article mentions that a number of executives are doing it." Well, the second executive can't wait to get to his telephone so he can order a herd of cattle. He is following the herd instinct not only figuratively but literally.

Another day, the "in" thing might be Lodestar Titanium, which "everyone" is buying because it's a cinch to double in price in six months.

Intelligent investing requires a considerable amount of analysis. Intelligent speculation—and I am not against speculation as long as the executive has first met his more important financial goals—requires perhaps even more analysis. Investing some money in Lodestar Titanium because of a fifth-hand rumor is not speculation—it is gambling. And you can probably get better odds at Las Vegas if you want to gamble.

There are literally hundreds of financial institutions ready and waiting to give an executive advice. He cannot delegate the job of personal financial planning to them because it is one job that is too important to delegate. But he can listen to their sales pitches and obtain the benefit of their analyses. Then he can make his own decisions.

Or he can go to one of the new personal financial counseling institutions that are opening up. These groups have no ax to grind. They advise on all sorts of investments, and their fee is not related to the type or volume of investments they select. Thus these groups don't get any richer by recommending cattle over mutual funds or oil wells over convertible debentures. The executive can therefore be assured a greater degree of objectivity in the advice he receives. But he still must make the final decision.

XIV

The Broader View of Management

*A*merica today finds itself embroiled in an urban crisis. Just as the Bible said it would, the sins of the fathers have finally caught up with the sons.

Many of the efforts of government to solve the urban crisis have ended in abject failure. The liberals of this country are in a state of disarray. All of a sudden a large part of the press and other opinion makers have turned to the businessman as the last major source of help, for business controls the jobs in this country— and more jobs for minority groups are what is needed. Whether he likes it or not, every businessman in this country has been thrust onto stage center.

I think that one of the reasons the country is putting an increasingly heavy reliance on business to help solve major social ills can be attributed to a growing awareness that pure idealism cannot work, but perhaps pragmatism can.

People will no doubt accuse me of being a cynic, but I happen to believe that there are very few true idealists in the world—people who want and get nothing for what they give. As far as I can recall, the last one died almost 2,000 years ago. Even your classic altruist usually gets something in return for his altruism: an immense amount of ego gratification.

So-called idealistic actions are rarely motivated by idealism. Usually, the individual does something to make himself feel good, to make a profit, or whatever. If, in order to accomplish these personal goals, he inadvertently helps someone else, that help does not constitute idealism. He has formed the basis of a symbiotic relationship, where both parties need each other to accomplish their own personal objectives.

Throughout history, individuals have been rather uneasy when confronted by a seemingly idealistic and unselfish act. The standard question has always been, "What's in it for you?" If the receiver discovers that the giver is benefited in some way by his apparently noble act, he is made more comfortable.

Now, business has in the past performed some seemingly idealistic acts. For many years, business has been one of the largest supporters of American higher education. Was this sacrificing of profits done out of selflessness, out of a burning belief that education for education's sake was worth supporting? Of course not.

At first, companies gave in response to pressures placed upon them by colleges and universities, by communities, and by alumni who were executives at those companies. After contributing in this manner for some years, a growing number of businessmen began to realize that they had a reason to support higher education which had nothing to do with pressure. They needed college graduates to help run their businesses. At first, support went to colleges and universities in and around the locations where the companies had facilities. Gradually, the support expanded to schools throughout the country. Idealism? Absolutely not. The companies began to discover that not all their executives were coming from those local schools.

This process is beginning to repeat itself in the handling of the urban crisis. Some businessmen are responding because of pressures placed upon them. Others, like the National Alliance of Businessmen, have moved past this stage. They have come to perceive that protecting their profits—indeed the profit-making system itself—requires that the social problems being experienced by Negroes and other minority groups be solved. They are even receiving government aid to attack these problems. There is very little idealism in these actions. It is plain old American-style pragmatism, and that is what is going to solve America's urban crisis.

Now, what can business really do?

First, it can provide training to bring disadvantaged

people "up to speed." One company I know of has developed a program called MIND to train semiliterate people quickly and inexpensively in reading, writing, and numerical skills. This company is no more idealistic than most. It expects to make a profit from this program.

Second, business must be willing to hire people into entry-level positions who formerly would not have met the company's qualifications. With some training and a little patience, many people with disadvantaged backgrounds can quickly become productive workers. Does the hiring of such people represent idealism? I don't think so. Business has of late been caught in a crunch between a great demand for skilled workers and a limited supply of such workers. It is in business's long-term interest to expand the labor pool to insure future growth.

Of course, Negroes and other minority group employees are usually not hired directly into skilled positions. For the most part they come in at the bottom of the organization and thereby free other people to move up the skills ladder. This is not an inequitable approach per se, in my opinion. I believe in the process of vertical osmosis. Given the opportunity, talent rises—seeps, if you will—through the organization. To the extent that minority group employees can join in this vertical osmosis, the urban crisis will be well on its way to resolution. But they must have the opportunity.

Providing that opportunity is the third thing business can do. Now, that doesn't mean "discriminating in reverse" and promoting a less qualified minority group employee over someone else who is more qualified. Discriminating in reverse is still a form of discrimination. What we are trying to do is eliminate discrimination, not perpetuate it in another form.

I am against discrimination, not primarily out of idealistic beliefs, but because it impedes the movement of the best qualified people to the top of the organization. If my company doesn't allow the best people to reach the top, it cannot by definition be as good—substitute the word "profitable," if you want to—as it might have been.

The way I see it, once a member of a minority group has been given the training to enable him to take an entry-level job, he is then on his own. If he never goes any further, he must look to himself for the reasons. But if he demonstrates the skills and motivation to advance, he *must* be given the opportunity to rise in the organization. There just aren't enough people with both talent *and* drive in this country that we can afford to overlook anyone.

If I were still heading a company, I would insist that each employee—no matter what the color of his skin, no matter what his religion—be given an equal chance at each and every promotional opportunity. And I would fire any manager who didn't carry out these policies both in letter and in the spirit. These managers would be discharged not because they were prejudiced, but because their prejudice cost my company some profits by permitting the second- or third-qualified individual, rather than the best-qualified, to get a responsible job.

A number of people have started to push "black capitalism" as the panacea for the country's social ills. I don't think black capitalism will work over the long run, but for the moment it is a worthwhile movement. There has been a history of prejudice in this country toward each new minority group. And each group has followed basically the same pattern on its road to integration. Denied the opportunity to advance in many companies, members of the minority group went into business for themselves. In so doing, they proved that they could manage a business as well as the next guy. Their success led many companies, which previously had denied them equality of opportunity, to reconsider and subsequently change their behavior. Eventually, many of these minority group businesses withered away, because they were not economically viable. But they served their purpose in demonstrating that no one group has the exclusive patent rights on talent.

The same role can be played by black capitalism. What Negroes need right now is a string of successes to prove that they too can manage a business as well as anyone else.

Therefore, I believe that companies and individual executives should help the black capitalist movement if that movement asks for help. By help, I am thinking

less of money and more of management expertise.
Many European writers a few years ago identified a
technology gap as the reason American business was so
much ahead of European business. On further examination, there is evidence that the technology gap—if
there is one—is not very wide. It is the management
gap that makes businesses in other countries less successful than those in the United States. We have
learned to manage. We have identified management
fundamentals and we have applied them. We have devised sophisticated control systems and increased the
autonomy of many managers.

To my way of thinking, the best help that can be
given to black capitalist entrepreneurs is advice and
counsel on how to be dynamic managers. This is a marvelous role for retired executives to play in the "repayment" phase of their lives—again, not because of in-
herent idealism, but because it makes these executives
useful and productive once more.

XV

Management's Challenges for the Future

*W*hen I was in college, I was a student assistant in the department of psychology and philosophy. One of my professors was a wonderful old gentleman by the name of Hasse Octavius Enwall.

My ambition at that time was to obtain a fellowship and eventually teach philosophy. I mentioned my dream to Professor Enwall, and one night he invited me to his home. "Mitchell," he said, "I understand your desire to teach, but have you any independent income?"

"No, sir, I don't. I'm working my way through college; that's why I'm a student assistant in your department."

"Well," he replied, "let me give you a piece of fatherly advice. Go out into the world and first get yourself on the right side of the ledger. Then come back and teach, not because you have to teach, but because you love to teach." And then he broke down in tears.

Nothing in my life has ever made a greater impression on me. I accepted Professor Enwall's advice and went out into the world of business. I placed myself on "the right side of the ledger," and now I am spending a great deal of time teaching, not because I have to teach, but because I love to teach.

But I discovered that business was something more than making money, although I won't deny the importance of remuneration. Business has always been terribly exciting to me. The process of establishing a goal, convincing others that it is a reasonable and attainable goal, and then managing a team to achieve that goal has been immensely gratifying and challenging. In short, it's been great fun.

The first challenge of management is to convey this sense of purpose—this fun—in business to a new generation of college students. These students are being assaulted on all sides by people who say, "Do something productive with your life. Go into the government. Go into the Peace Corps. Make a social contribution. Don't go into business and soil your hands with filthy profits." Businessmen—in what must be one of the few times in their lives—sit idly by and don't respond to this criticism.

Who says we don't make a contribution? We contribute those so-called filthy profits which have made this the most affluent society in the world—affluent enough to allow some people to spend a great deal of time attacking our affluence.

The United States government is supposed to be the richest in the world, but it has not one single penny of its own. In fact, its debt–equity ratio is enough to make any prudent businessman seriously contemplate suicide. Ultimately, the government gets its money from profits. Profits provide an incentive for money to be invested. Investments create jobs. The salaries that are paid to millions of workers and the profits that are left over are taxed by the government. Even the communist countries in one way or another make profits. Where else do they get funds to run their governments and to make investments?

To me, business has a definite social purpose. We've got to get our message across to young people so that we can get our fair share of the talent in the upcoming generation.

A number of academicians who previously dealt in facts have turned their hand to social prophecy. Looking ahead to the year 2000, they see a society so efficient that only a small percentage of the population will be needed to produce all the goods and services we will require. Since the majority of the population that will not be working cannot be allowed to starve, the government or some other agency will see that they are paid for doing nothing. The prophets say that the consequence of this course of action will be the destruction of the Protestant ethic.

Although these sophisticated articles are filled with all sorts of technological jargon and Buck Rogers predictions, they are awfully reminiscent of what I was reading during the 1930's. The word "computer" hadn't been invented yet, but no matter. The word "automation" was just as useful. Automation was also going to destroy the Protestant ethic—millions of people were already out of work and millions more soon would be.

The problem was that the prophets of that time couldn't envision all the new products and services that would come to be offered. The computer alone has probably created far more jobs than it has destroyed. There are thousands of unfilled openings for programmers, to mention but one new occupation created by the computer.

I think our current prophets also suffer from tunnel vision. I don't know what the new goods and services of the year 2000 will be, but I am confident that there will be plenty of them and therefore plenty of jobs also.

There's no question, however, that we are living in a world of increasingly accelerating change. The only constant we can rely upon is that nothing is constant. Therein lies a major challenge for management.

Change can be mastered only if it can be responded to quickly. As a result, a good deal more decentralization and delegation of decision making is going to have to occur. The company that persists in keeping a tight rein on decisions and the company that defers decisions to large committees is going to miss every opportunity that comes along. For each challenge that change hurls also contains the seeds of opportunity. Those companies that delegate decision making to the very lowest level at which such decisions can be made intelligently will have the ability to move fast and seize opportunities before their competitors.

Greater decentralization must go hand in hand with greater control. Fortunately, management tools such as the computer have come along—not to control anything, because computers can't even control themselves without the aid of programmers, but to provide faster and more reliable indicators as to whether the company's built-in controls are functioning as they should be. These more sophisticated management tools are going to require more sophisticated managers. The fundamentals of management will remain unchanged, but tomorrow's manager will have to have a better technical background in order to apply them.

Another challenge that managers face today and will continue to face in the future is to obtain the best possible return on the assets in their businesses. The "conglomerate" movement has shortened the interval between the time when capital is utilized inefficiently and the time when the penalty must be paid for such poor performance. Essentially, I think the growing number of acquisitions being made by companies today is a healthy development, so long as it is truly aimed at achieving maximum utilization of capital resources. Of course, some acquisitions are made to bleed a company of its resources and not to improve the use of these resources. These will have to be curtailed, and there are concrete indications that Congress is going to do just that. Nevertheless, tomorrow's top managers are going to have to do a better and better job if they want to remain top managers.

The future will also bring accelerated pressure to share the results of company success not only with the company's executives but with all its employees. Many companies now have profit-sharing plans, and the number with some form of profit sharing will increase dramatically over the next few decades. Unions, which historically opposed profit-sharing and company stock plans as tricks by management to win the loyalty of the workers, have begun to change their outlook under pressure from their members because of the outstanding rewards that many of these plans have produced.

Critics of hourly profit-sharing and stock-purchase plans have argued that the top management group really controls the amount of profits to be made, and hourly employees can have little impact on corporate earnings. Certainly, one hourly employee cannot affect a company's profits to the same extent as a top manager. But all hourly employees taken together constitute the great bulk of the company's payroll costs and a very large percentage of its total costs. If these employees can be motivated to increase their productivity even a little and to waste just a little less raw material, the results can have a staggeringly good impact on the profit and loss statement.

We had a profit-sharing plan at one company I headed. When profits were good, the total compensation of hourly employees was significantly higher than any other employer around. Even when profits were poor, total compensation was still competitive. If nothing else, that profit-sharing plan gave us an edge on the competition in getting the best and most motivated workers. Their presence, in turn, contributed materially to the success of the company—and to their own financial success as well.

More and more, hourly workers are going to want a piece of the action, and it is high time they got it.

The current challenges that management faces in helping to resolve the urban crisis have already been discussed. I would be remiss, however, in not listing the eradication of discrimination and the provision of equal opportunity as challenges for the future. For these goals will be with us for a long while.

One consequence of this country's increasing prosperity is the growing number of young people who are inheriting substantial sums of money. I am somewhat ambivalent concerning this development. On the one hand, I have always wanted to provide for my children, as any father would. On the other hand, I am worried as to the effects of inheritance. Too often, I have seen young people of great promise sit on their hands and spend the old man's money. In earlier times, there weren't enough of such playboys to make a great difference, and eventually many of them spent themselves into a job anyway. Now, however, we have developed the capacity in this country to produce hundreds of thousands of playboys.

Frankly, I don't know what the answer is. I do know, however, that there will continue to be a demand—a constantly growing demand—for outstanding managers. And to be outstanding in tomorrow's management world is going to take a lot more talent and drive than is required today. Today's outstanding managers will be considered mediocre by tomorrow's standards, just as yesterday's outstanding managers would be considered mediocre by today's standards.

In the past, we have solved many major problems because they just had to be solved. I hope we can also solve the problem of providing sufficient motivated raw material for the management teams of tomorrow.

❋　　❋　　❋　　❋

Fun, to me, is facing a challenge and overcoming it. My career as a manager, for all its hard work, was never anything but fun. I enjoyed myself immensely. And as my successors confront their challenges, both old and new, I wish them the same enjoyment, the same fun, that comes from establishing a goal and leading others to its attainment—that comes from being a manager.

Index

acting manager, meaning of, 60-61
Albert, Frankie, 30
assistant manager, as title, 61

Bannister, Roger, 21-22
black capitalism, 177-178
board chairman, president as, 143
board of directors
  composition of, 158-161
  outside members of, 159-161
  responsibilities of, 158
  retirement from, 163
  role of, 157-171
  salaries for, 162-163
  stockholders and, 157
  as team, 30
Bok, Edward, 153
bonus plans, 114-118
  deferred, 124-125
  discretionary, 122
  distribution in, 118-119
  group incentive and, 120-121

secrecy in, 123
  see also compensation
budget, control through, 81-82, 89-93
business, social purpose of, 181-182
Business Week, 146

closure, psychological meaning of, 54
commissions, as compensation, 112-115
committees
  decisions by, 37
  formation of, 36
communication, 98-108
  face-to-face, 102-103
  by president, 98-100
  rumors and, 101
  see also employee house organ
compensation, 109-133
  bonus plans and, 115-118
  commissions and, 112-114
  deferred, 124-125
  for directors, 162-163
  as motivation, 109-110

compensation (*cont.*)
  paternalism and, 125-126
  profit and, 112, 117
  salary increases and, 129-131
  status and, 132-133
  stock options as, 127-128
  titles and, 131-133
conglomerate movement, 183-184
control
  budget and, 81-82, 89-93
  delegation and, 80-82
  engineering and, 94-97
  operations review in, 94
  reports and, 96
  of research, 92-94
  statistical indicators in, 83, 86-87
  through subordinate managers, 83-84
  techniques of, 80-97
  of unit cost, 84-85
corporate staff
  role of, 134-141
  size of, 140
cost control, 84-85
cost reduction, as organization goal, 27-28

death benefits, planning of, 166-167
decentralization
  defined, 39
  delegation and, 38-47
  profit and loss responsibility and, 46
  subordinate and, 42-44
  transfer pricing and, 46-47
decision making
  control and, 88-89, 183

delegation and, 38-47
  management team and, 51-52
  by president, 150-151
deferred compensation, 124-125
delegation
  contraindication in, 49
  control and, 80-82
  decentralization and, 38-47
  failure in, 76-77
  fear of, 88
directors, board of, see board of directors
disadvantaged people, hiring and training of, 174-178
dismissals and removals, 62-64
dividend policy, president's role in, 148-149
division manager, profit and loss responsibility of, 46
dream goal, 18
  see also goals

employee house organ, 102
  president's use of, 104
employee meetings, 99-101
employees, communication with, 98-108
engineering, control of costs in, 94-97
engineering supervisor, background of, 54
Enwall, Hasse Octavius, 179-180
executive
  dismissal or transfer of, 62-64
  life insurance for, 168-169
  personal finances of, 163-170

retirement of, 153, 163-170
see also executive vice-president; manager; president
executive searchers, 67
executive vice-president
  as successor to president, 155-156
  transfer of, 64-65

feedback, in training programs, 72-73
financial planning, for executives, 164-171
five-year plan, sales, 25-26

goals
  believers and, 19
  cost reduction as, 27-28
  establishing of, 17-27
  group advice on, 20-21
  in pectore, 18
  leadership and, 31
  organization and, 31
  planning of, 21-23
  position description and, 32-33
  return on investment as, 26-27
  teamwork and, 30-31
  types of, 26-27
Golden Rule, 12
graphology, 49, 52
group advice, in goal setting, 20-21
group incentive plans, 120-121

Harvard Business School, 75
home, cost and upkeep of, 165

incentive plans, 112-113, 120-121

information, employees' need for, 100-102
  see also communication
in-house talent, for management team, 55

leadership
  goals and, 31
  organization and, 29-30
life insurance, 164-165
  "adequate" amount of, 168-169

management
  activities of, 16
  broader view of, 172-178
  college graduates and, 174
  defined, 14
  fundamentals of, 12
  future challenges for, 179-186
  sense of purpose in, 180-182
management team
  candidates for, 77
  as capital asset, 56-57
  compensation for, 109-133
  decision making and, 51-52
  delegation and, 49
  dismissals from, 62-64
  in-house talent for, 55-56
  outside talent for, 55, 60
  personnel problems in, 62-66
  replacement planning and, 58
  selection of, 48-68
  semiannual inventory of, 57-58
  subordinates and, 50-52

manager
    acting or assistant, 61
    aggressive, 52
    background of, 54
    decision making by, 38-42
    delegation by, 42-47
    discharge or removal of, 62-64
    future need for, 186
    goal establishing by, 17-27
    line vs. staff, 135-138
    number of people reporting to, 35
    qualifications of, 14-15
    selection of, 53-54
    subordinate and, 42-44, 50-52
    training role of, 69-79
    see also management; management team; president
manpower planning
    need for, 57
    replacement planning and, 58-59
Massachusetts Institute of Technology, 75
mergers, challenge of, 183-184
merit increase, 130
minorities, hiring and training of, 174-177
mistakes, decentralization and, 44-46
money
    as prime motivator, 11
    compensation and, see compensation
    see also salary increases
motivation, compensation as, 109-110

Namath, Joe, 30

National Alliance of Businessmen, 174
Negroes
    black capitalism and, 177-178
    hiring and training of, 174-177

one-upmanship, 98
operations review meeting, 94
orchestra, as symbol of organization, 33
organization
    control of, 80-97; see also control
    defined, 29
    goals of, 17-27
    leadership and, 29-30
    position descriptions and, 33-35
    teamwork and, 30-31
outside talent, search for, 55, 60
overhead, control of, 89-90

Peace Corps, 180
performance appraisal, criteria for, 74-76
personal financial planning, 164-171
personnel management, careers in, 14-15
personnel problems, on management team, 62-66
PERT (program evaluation and review technique), 11
phrenology, 49, 52
planning
    goal-setting and, 21-23
    long-range, 24-25
    manpower, 57-59

position description
  goals and, 32-35
  organization and, 33-35
president
  as board chairman, 143
  as chief executive officer,
    142-143
  communication with, 98-
    100
  community relations of, 146-
    147
  corporate staff and, 134-141
  decentralization by, 38-40
  decision making of, 38-42,
    150
  delegation of responsibility
    by, 38-47
  dividend policy of, 147-149
  duties and responsibilities
    of, 142-156
  face-to-face communication
    with, 103
  failure to delegate, 76-77
  financial relations of, 147-
    148
  life plan of, 154
  management team and, 48-
    68
  as manager, 147
  public and, 106-108
  qualities of, 151-153
  replacement of, 77-78, 154-
    155
  requests from, 151-153
  retirement of, 153
  socializing by, 104-105
  successor to, 154-155
  telephone answering by,
    104
  training for, 77-78
  yes men and, 52

Presidents Association, 75-76
president's office, concept of,
  144-145
profit, compensation and, 112,
  117
profit and loss, delegation of
  responsibility for, 45-46
profit improvement, as organization goal, 28
profit-sharing plans, 183-185
prosperity, dangers of, 185-
  186
psychological tests, 13, 52
public relations, president and,
  106-108
purpose, of organization or
  business, 180-181

replacement planning, for
  management team, 58
research, control of, 92-94
responsibility, delegation of,
  38-47
retirement, from board of directors, 163
retirement plans, for manager
  or president, 154, 165-
  167
return on investment, as long-
  term goal, 27-28
rumors, communication and,
  101

salary increases, planned, 129-
  131
salary rates, establishment of,
  109-133
sales management, careers in,
  14-15
salesmen, staff men as, 135

secrets, vs. communication, 102

Simpson, O. J., 30

skill inventories, 56

social contribution, need for, 180-181

socializing, executive, 105-106

staff man, vs. line, 134-141

Stanford University, 75

statistical indicators, 83, 86-87

status, as compensation, 132-133

stockholders
board of directors and, 157
company goals and, 27-28

stock option plans, 127-129, 184

subordinate
decision making by, 42-43, 50
feedback from, 73-74
ideal, 53
on management team, 50-52
profit and loss responsibility of, 45-46
training of, 72-74

subordinate manager, control through, 83-84

teamwork, 30; *see also* management team

telephone answering, by president, 104

titles
compensation and, 131-133
meaningless, 61

Tittle, Y. A., 30

training
feedback in, 72-74
manager's role in, 69-79
performance appraisal in, 74-76
subordinate and, 72-74

transfer pricing, 46-47

unit cost, control of, 84-85

vice-president, transfer or removal of, 64-66
see also executive vice-president

Wall Street Journal, 146

yes man, vs. aggressive manager, 52